The New York State Constitutional Convention of 1915 and the Modern State Governor.

THOMAS SCHICK
New York University

National Municipal League 1978

LC Catalog Number 78-58213
Copyright 1978 Thomas Schick
All rights reserved

Printed by Sowers Printing Company
Lebanon, Pennsylvania

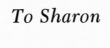

To Sharon

Acknowledgments

I should like to express my gratitude to several people who helped to make this work possible. First and foremost, my thanks go to Dr. Charlton F. Chute, Professor Emeritus of the New York University Graduate School of Public Administration. Dr. Chute was a constant source of wise counsel and encouragement throughout the entire period of my research and writing, and I am deeply indebted to him. Dr. Troy R. Westmeyer, also of the Graduate School, gave much appreciated advice and support at various stages of the study. Dr. Abraham L. Gitlow, Dean of NYU's College of Business and Public Administration, provided a great deal of encouragement and assistance, and many kindnesses. Dr. Israel M. Kirzner, Professor of Economics at the NYU Graduate School of Arts and Science, was an enormously supportive friend and counselor to a grateful junior associate.

A commanding figure in the New York State Constitutional Convention of 1915 was Henry L. Stimson, and the study draws heavily on the Henry L. Stimson Papers at Yale University. I greatly appreciate the warm interest shown in the study by McGeorge Bundy, President of the Ford Foundation and co-author with Stimson of the latter's memoirs, and I am honored by the foreword that he has been kind enough to write.

The study could not have been published without the support of the National Municipal League.

Finally, I want to thank my wife Sharon, for her help, offered in numberless ways, her encouragement from beginning to end, and not least, her infinite patience.

Foreword

When I reported to Henry L. Stimson, in 1946, to assist in the preparation of his memoirs, I had never heard of the New York Constitutional Convention of 1915. It was a gap in my knowledge that Colonel Stimson did his energetic best to fill during the months that followed. His life had included many dramatic and demanding experiences, but there was none that he recalled with greater clarity and warmth than that Convention. In our book we tried to do justice to the Convention, and a further and better effort was made by Elting Morison a decade later. But we were handicapped, as all other students have been, by the absence of any solid history of the Convention as a whole—its antecedents, its life, and its eventual consequences. Given the importance of the Convention, not only in the lives of its participants but in the life of New York State, this omission is hard to explain except as a consequence of the vulgar error that confuses failure at the polls with unimportance.

Fortunately the error has now been corrected by Thomas Schick. As one who covered the same ground 30 years ago, much more lightly and hastily, and from only one man's standpoint, I am deeply impressed by his achievement. It is a major contribution to the understanding of a seminal event in the history of the government of the states. In sponsoring its publication the National Municipal League adds one more to its long list of services in the cause of better state and local government. McGEORGE BUNDY
June 1978

vii

Table of Contents

Introduction

The executive branch of the New York State government is organized into 20 central departments. The heads of these departments are, for the most part, appointed by the governor and can be removed by him. Only three other state officials are elected along with the governor. They are: the lieutenant governor, the comptroller, and the attorney general. Among the most prominent functions the governor is charged with is the formulation and presentation of a comprehensive state budget.

These salient features of the state's executive branch are today not only accepted as appropriate and desirable, they are acknowledged to be essential to the effective administration of a modern state government. This was not always the case. Fifty years ago the executive branch consisted of over 180 departments, offices, boards and commissions, the heads of which were selected in widely varying ways. In addition to the offices of governor, lieutenant governor, comptroller, and attorney general, those of state treasurer, secretary of state, and state engineer were elective. As to the governor's budget-making function, his input into the budgeting process was minimal.

The consolidation of administrative agencies, the shortening of the state ballot, and the adoption of an executive budget date from the years 1926-27, in which two amendments to the state constitution were passed providing for these reforms. But the process which culminated in the reorganization of the state's executive branch, as these reforms are collectively referred to, began well before that—in the New York State Constitutional Convention of 1915. The delegates to that convention produced a constitution which offered, in Leonard D. White's phrase, "a remarkable forecast of modern tendencies"[1] in its provisions for the executive branch. It proposed a revolutionary reorganization of the executive based on the three principles of consolidation of administrative agencies, a short ballot, and an executive budget. The proposed constitution was defeated, but its impact is commonly acknowledged by scholars of state government and reorganization to have nevertheless been enormous. This impact lay in the discussion and debate in the convention and in the subsequent campaign for ratification which created a new popular awareness of the issue of reorganization—an awareness formerly limited to a relative handful of reformers—and which began a process of public education on the need for reorganization. It was this discussion and debate which was judged by Finla G. Crawford to have "had a marked effect in making possible the adoption of administrative reorganization eleven years later,"[2] and which, together with other aspects of the convention, was judged by Frederick C. Mosher to have ". . . provided the ideological fodder and stimulated the reformist fervor for most of the significant changes in New York State government in the next three decades."[3]

Nor was the impact of the convention confined to New York State. The reorganization it proposed was a revolutionary one not only by New York's standards, but by those of every other state as well. It is therefore not surprising that its proposal, in Walter F. Dodd's words, "attracted the attention of the country,"[4] and that it engendered discussion and debate far beyond the borders of New York State. As in New York, it was through this discussion and debate that the convention had, in the judgment of Arthur Eugene Buck and Frederick A. Cleveland, "a marked influence on the political thinking of the whole country"[5] on the subject of state executive reorganization.

The impact the convention had in helping to make possible the reorganization of the executive in New York and in other states earned it a special place in the literature of reorganization. Virtually every study of executive reorganization refers to it as one of the earliest steps taken toward such reorganization, with one scholar, Arthur N. Holcombe, stating simply that "there is no better . . . starting point for a study of the problem of reform in state administration than the work of the [1915] New York convention."[6] Yet, despite this universal acknowledgement of the significance of the convention, nowhere in the copious literature of reorganization is there to be found a full-length, indepth treatment of this important event.[7] Nowhere is there any work which focuses on the convention in an attempt to address in detail such fundamental questions as how the convention came to be a forum for discussion of executive reorganization, a subject about which most people at the time were ignorant; who was responsible for the convention's concentration on reorganization proposals and for their ultimate acceptance by the convention; whether there was any substantial resistance in the convention to these proposals and, if there was, how such resistance was overcome; and, finally, why the proposed constitution with its reorganization features failed to secure ratification by the voters. In short, nowhere has the best "starting point for a study of the problem of reform in state administration" itself ever been closely examined.

It is the objective of this study to fill this void in the otherwise well known story of reorganization. The study presents a description and analysis of the convention and its contribution to reorganization. It offers detailed answers to the aforementioned fundamental questions and to many others concerning the convention and its work, and, in so doing, helps to clarify just why the convention is considered to have been an important early step toward reorganization.

The study is divided into four main sections. In order to appreciate the revolutionary nature and the significance of the convention's work, it is essential to place it into historical context and to examine the background against which it took place. The first section, dealing with the development of the state executive from 1776 up to the eve of the convention and the modest beginnings of the reorganization movement in the latter part of this period, with an emphasis on this development and these beginnings in New York State, provides this context and background. The second section deals with the preparation for the convention. It was this preparation which set the focus and established the tone of the convention, thereby determining the course of its work, and an examination of this preparation is necessary for a proper understanding of the convention itself. The third section focuses on the convention itself, from the selection of convention officers and the designation of committee assignments, through committee work and the convention debates, to final approval of the proposed constitution. The fourth section deals with the campaign for ratification, concentrating chiefly on how it was conducted and why it failed. A brief fifth section adds an epilogue which recounts in summary fashion how and when reorganization was ultimately realized in New York State and touches on the reorganization activity in other states in the wake of the convention, fuller accounts of both of which are available in the literature of reorganization.

A note on sources. Excepting the first section, for which both ample and excellent secondary sources were available,[8] the study relied principally on official documents of the convention, writings of and recorded oral histories by convention delegates and others closely associated with the convention's work, printed propaganda utilized by the proponents and the foes of reorganization in the campaign for ratification, and newspaper articles and journal and magazine pieces of the period. For background material the study relied on standard works on state government, writings on reorganization, histories of New York, and biographies—and in one case an autobiography—of the leading convention delegates. Further background material was acquired through interviews with several persons who were either active in the reorganization movement at that time or who were familiar with the thinking and the work of some of the principal delegates.

The two most helpful groups of sources were collected papers of and recorded oral histories by delegates. Such collections as the Henry L. Stimson Papers (Yale University), the Elihu Root Papers (Library of Congress), and the Frederick C. Tanner Papers (Columbia University), among others, are rich mines of information about early twentieth century New York State government and politics, and the reorganization movement of that period. The same is true of the recorded oral histories by Frederick C. Tanner and John Lord O'Brian, among others in Columbia University's Oral History Research Office. More than any other sources or group of sources, it was these, used in conjunction with the general sources cited earlier, which helped develop the perspective of the New York State Constitutional Convention of 1915 offered in this study.

NOTES

[1]Leonard D. White, *Trends in Public Administration* (New York: McGraw-Hill Book Co., Inc., 1933), p. 178.

[2]Alexander C. Flick, ed., *History of the State of New York*, 10 vols. (New York: Columbia University Press, 1935), vol. 7: *Constitutional Developments 1867-1915*, by Finla G. Crawford, p. 231.

[3]Frederick C. Mosher, "The Executive Budget, Empire State Style," *Public Administration Review* 12 (Spring 1952):78.

[4]Walter F. Dodd, "State Administrative Reorganization in New York," *American Bar Association Journal* 12 (July 1926):455.

[5]Arthur E. Buck, and F. A. Cleveland, *The Budget and Responsible Government,* with an Introduction by William Howard Taft (New York: The MacMillan Co., 1920), p. 109.

[6]Arthur N. Holcombe, review of *The Development of the Power of the State Executive, With Special Reference to the State of New York,* by Margaret C. Alexander, in *National Municipal Review,* November 1917, p. 753.

[7]As is reflected in the bibliography beginning on p. 137, several articles on the convention did appear in scholarly journals in the years 1915-16. However, these were uniformly brief, relatively superficial, and often incomplete accounts.

[8]Foremost among these is Leslie Lipson's classic, *The American Governor from Figurehead to Leader* (Chicago: University of Chicago Press, 1939).

Chapter 1

Development of the Office
of Governor to 1915

From detested minion of Royal power, to stepson of legislative
domination, to popular figurehead, to effective executive is the
story of the American Governor.[1]

As this capsule view of the development of the office of
governor suggests, this development took place in several distinct
stages. The stages have been identified[2] as: (1) 1776-1789, from the
period in which the states began formulating and adopting their
first constitutions, to the year in which the national constitution was
ratified; (2) 1789-1850, the latter year selected not because of its
significance per se, but because it represents the mid point between the prevailing trends in the first and second halves of the
century; (3) 1850-1917, the latter being the year in which the first
comprehensive state government reorganization was implemented;
and (4) 1917 to the present. While these dates mark the development of the governorship throughout all the states and would,
therefore, vary slightly when focusing on this development within
specific states, they provide a useful framework for a general
overview and, with the exception of the 1917 date, for which we
will substitute 1915, the discussion will proceed within this
framework.

1

DEVELOPMENT OF THE OFFICE OF GOVERNOR

1776-1789

Two dominant characteristics of the structure of the early state governments as articulated in their first constitutions were a commitment to the doctrine of separation of powers, though, as will be seen, it was a curious "separation" they effectuated, and a weak executive branch. Allegiance to a strict separation of powers was explicitly referred to by six of the constitutions. Massachusetts' constitution, for example, stated with unmistakable clarity that:

> ... the legislative department shall never exercise the executive and judicial powers, or either of them; the executive shall never exercise the legislative and judicial powers, or either of them; the judicial shall never exercise the legislative and executive powers, or either of them. ....[3]

This emphasis on a division of powers was, of course, a direct and understandable reaction against the concentration of power in the Royal Governors in most of the states prior to the Revolution. These Royal Governors called, adjourned, and dissolved colonial assemblies at will, appointed military, civil, and judicial officials, exercised an absolute pardoning power, and, in their capacities as commanders in chief, commanded the state militia. The first step, thus, in ensuring a separation of powers was the drastic diminution of the power of the executive. And, with some variations, that is what the first constitutions did.

In the first constitutions of the majority of states, executive councils were associated with the governor, and in four states— New Hampshire, Pennsylvania, Delaware, and Massachusetts— "there was not even a governor at all in the ordinary sense,"[4] with the real executive consisting of a council. In no state did the governor possess an independent and unqualified veto over legislation. Nowhere did he adjourn the legislature, and in the few states which allowed prorogation, such as New York, there were strict limits placed on that right. Nowhere did the governor have the power to appoint even one officer independently of another body. Nowhere was the governor's term more than three years, and only in New York and Delaware was it three, with South Carolina deciding on two, and the rest of the states on one. Finally, in four states— Pennsylvania, Delaware, South Carolina, and New Hampshire— the term governor wasn't even used; instead, the reference was to a less sinister-sounding "president" or "president and commander in chief."

New York's constitution provided for a relatively stronger executive.[5] His three-year term, his veto power, albeit shared with others, and his exclusive right to grant pardons except in capital offenses, all combined to enhance the status of New York's governor over that of the average state governor. Measured by any other standard, however, even New York's governor was, in Leslie Lipson's phrase, "far from robust."[6] New York, after all, had, under its colonial governor, "probably the most unfortunate government, a government arbitrary, corrupt, and inefficient,"[7] and it too wanted to check its executive. The prime means by which this was accomplished was by joining the governor with several others in a Council of Revision in the exercise of his veto, and in a Council of Appointment in the exercise of his power of appointment. The Council of Revision consisted of the governor, the chancellor, and three judges of the Supreme Court, with the power to veto legislation invested in a combination of the governor and any two of the others. The Council of Appointment consisted of the governor and four senators and it appointed officers throughout the state whose manner of appointment was not prescribed in the constitution.[8] Both were effective checks on the authority of the governor.

The executives fashioned by the great majority of the first state constitutions were weak and ineffectual. The states had well succeeded in cutting down the position they saw as the heir to the despised Royal Governors. Instead of the executives, the state legislatures, which, it was thought, were more subject to public control, now became the dominant political forces in the states. They were given far greater powers than the governors and were considered the focus of government in the states. In order to emphasize further the relative status of the governor and the legislature, it was the legislature and not the electorate at large which voted for governor in most of the states.[9]

If this transfer of the bulk of the governing powers from the executive to the legislative branch seems inconsistent with the states' ostensible commitment to a system based on a separation of powers, it is because the ideal of separation had, in fact, been abandoned. Having pledged themselves to a separation of powers it would have been appropriate for the states to dilute the hitherto absolute powers of the executive and distribute those powers more or less evenly between the several branches of government. What they actually did was emasculate the executive and trade an all-powerful governor for an all-powerful legislature. This failure to construct a true separation of powers was noted by at least two contemporary observers. Madison, speaking in the Constitutional

Convention of 1787, described the distribution of power in the states:

> Experience had proved a tendency in our governments to throw all power into the legislative vortex. The executives of the states are in general little more than ciphers; the legislatures are omnipotent.[10]

Madison decried this situation when, in *Federalist 47*, he articulated the principle of separation of powers as having been designed to prevent the tyranny of any one branch of government, legislative or executive:

> . . . the accumulation of all powers, legislative, executive and judiciary in the same hands, whether of one, a few or many, and whether hereditary, self-appointed, or elective, may justly be pronounced the very definition of tyranny.[11]

Jefferson, complaining of the concentration of power in the legislature in his home state, wrote:

> All the powers of government, legislative, executive, and judiciary result to the legislative body. The concentrating [sic] these in the same hands is precisely the definition of despotic government. It will be no alleviation that these powers will be exercised by a plurality of hands, and not by a single one. One hundred seventy-three [the number of members of the Virginia legislature] despots would surely be as oppressive as one.[12]

It is not difficult to find an explanation for the abandonment by the states of the principle to which they had paid verbal allegiance. Madison, in *Federalist 47*, wrote:

> I wish not to be regarded as an advocate for the particular organization of the several state governments. I am fully aware that among the many and excellent principles which they exemplify, they carry strong marks of the haste, and still stronger of the inexperience, under which they are framed.[13]

Thus, in Madison's view, the inadequacies and inconsistencies of the state governments, such as the contradiction between their outspoken preference for a government in which power was divided and their de facto abandonment of this principle, are explainable by their inexperience and the pressures of time.[14] While the states recognized the value of a separation of powers, they were first and foremost determined to fashion a government which in no way would resemble the one they experienced under the colonial governors. "It was," after all, "on the executive branch essentially that the colonists waged their war of independence."[15] Part of that war was waged in the framing of the new executives. Their inexperience made them "unable to distinguish properly between a Crown governor and a popularly elected governor,"[16] and they hadn't the time to reflect on the difference. Had they been able to make this distinction they would have found it possible to design a separation of powers. As it happened, they neutralized the executive and separation of powers fell by the wayside.

1789-1850

That the first state constitutions and their provisions for the executive branch were the products of haste and inexperience is further reflected by the fact that soon after the end of the Revolutionary War, in an atmosphere of relative calm and with the benefit of several years experience, the states set about to revise their constitutions and their arrangements for the executive. Even during the Revolution, many had already begun to have second thoughts about the system of legislative domination they had fashioned as the system failed to respond adequately to a number of wartime incidents.[17] The coming of peace afforded people the opportunity to reflect on their experience and on the possibility of distinguishing between a Crown Governor and one of their own choice. The post-war period also saw a rapid decline of confidence in the legislatures, a decline which was to continue and grow throughout the end of the eighteenth and through the nineteenth centuries. This decline in confidence stemmed from the fact that many legislators were unable, or unwilling, to respond to the needs of the state as a whole, insisting instead on concerning themselves with their own narrow district or interest. While such a posture may have been appropriate in the colonial period when the legislature needed to protect local interests from a government, personified by a Royal Governor, which was preoccupied with imperial interests, it was not appropriate for a body to whom people looked for statewide governance. Arthur Holcombe explains:

> During the colonial period, when the responsibility for the conduct of government rested mainly on the executive, the predominance of local interests in the legislative branch served as a salutory check upon the executive tendency to prefer imperial to local interests of any sort. But when the sovereignty passed from the crown to the people, the legislature became the chief representative of the new sovereign, and the predominance of local and private interests signified the subversion of the general public interest.[18]

The consequences of this failure to govern the state as a whole, adds Holcombe, were "sufficiently disastrous to the common welfare to produce a general reaction against the original system of unchecked legislative supremacy."[19]

In addition to these general factors, an important specific spur to revision of the original state constitutions' provisions for the executive was the national Constitutional Convention of 1787. The debates in the convention reflected the concern and debate in the states over the proper role of the executive. When the convention adopted a scheme providing for a strong national executive in a system of real separation of powers, it provided the states with a concrete example of an alternative arrangement for their executives.[20] For this reason, 1789, the year in which the national constitution was ratified, is viewed as a significant date in the development of the state governor. Byron Abernathy writes:

> The adoption of the Constitution of the United States in 1789 marked the beginning of a new trend in the position of the state executive, as the example of balanced government and a relatively strong executive for the federal government exerted its influence on the states.[21]

The revisions of the state constitutional provisions for the executive in this period focused on four main areas: (1) abolition of the executive councils, (2) wider acceptance of an executive veto, (3) lengthening of the governor's term, and (4) popular election of the governor. Perhaps most symbolic of the beginning of the movement to make the executive an independent and co-equal branch of government, was the trend away from attaching executive councils to the governor. Georgia abolished its executive council in 1789 and was followed by South Carolina and Pennsylvania in 1790, and by Delaware in 1792. With the exception of Maine, none of the newly admitted states included an executive council in their governments. New York, which, of course, had no general council, did have a Council of Appointment which succeeded in hamstringing the governor in the crucial area of appointments. The Constitutional Convention of 1821, in a thorough review of the original constitution, abolished this council. From its inception the council had been the focus of great political intrigue and controversy.[22] The original constitution hadn't bothered to specify whether it was the governor alone who could make nominations with confirmation lying in the hands of the council, or whether the power to nominate was held equally by the governor and members of the council.[23] In 1801 a special convention called by the legislature decided that the power was indeed vested equally in the governor and the council members. As the patronage was quite extensive, consisting at one point of as many as 6,663 civil and 8,286 military offices,[24] the council and governor were almost constantly at odds with each other. In a speech opening the legislature on November 7, 1820, Governor George Clinton complained, with full justification, that:

If the ingenuity of man had been exercised to organize the appointing power in such a way as to produce continual intrigue and commotion in the state, none could have been devised with more effect than the present arrangement.[25]

In its 102-to-0 vote abolishing the council, the 1821 convention confirmed Clinton's assessment.[26]

The first states to revise their constitutions after the adoption of the federal constitution were Georgia in 1789 and Pennsylvania in 1790. Both adopted an executive veto in their revisions. New Hampshire gave its governor the veto in 1792 and in the same year the first western state admitted to the union, Kentucky, did so as well. While different, and in many cases qualified, forms of executive vetoes were adopted in this period, some form of veto was adopted by the great majority of states and, by 1850, few of the new and only six of the original states were without an executive veto of some kind. In New York, the Constitutional Convention of 1821 abolished the Council of Revision which shared the veto with the governor, and granted the whole of this power to the governor.

The terms of the governors were increased in this period from one to two, three, and four years. Georgia went in 1789 from a one- to a two-year term, and Pennsylvania, in 1790, from one to three years. Among the new states, Kentucky (1792) adopted a four-year term; Indiana (1816), a three-year term; and Illinois (1818), a four-year term. New York's Constitutional Convention of 1821, in what must be seen as an effort to counterbalance the general expansion of executive power it provided for,[27] cut back the governor's term from three to two years, but such a move was a singular exception to the rule.

Direct popular election of the governor became widely accepted. Pennsylvania in 1790 and Delaware in 1792 were among the first to include this in their revisions, with many of the states following suit shortly thereafter. Only a few of the original states delayed in adopting popular election—Virginia waited until 1850 and South Carolina, the last to yield, did so in 1866—and no new states admitted after 1800 adopted legislative election.

These changes represented the beginnings of the emancipation of the executive from legislative domination. The process of emancipation continued throughout the first half of the nineteenth century as the early criticism of the localism of the legislatures hardened into popular disenchantment over their continuing, and worsening, parochialism and corruption. By 1850, "legislative supremacy had disappeared,"[28] and the executive had become "a coordinate, as opposed to a subordinate branch of government."[29]

While the growth in the stature of the executive was appreciable when measured against the original relative roles and functions of the legislature and executive, it could not be said that the governor's office had become a powerful one or that he had become the focal point of state government. The old suspicions of executive authority were much too strong to allow this to happen and a concommitant development in this period effectively precluded it. This development, which, in time, proved to be one of the greatest obstacles to the development of the power of the governor, was the growth of the demand for popular government through increasing the number of elective, as opposed to appointive, public offices. The demand for such popular control of government had been growing from the immediate post-Revolutionary War period, and it reached its high point in the 1830s with the advent of Jacksonian Democracy. The "Jacksonian dogma," as it is referred to by its critics,[30] held that as control of government is exercised by the people through periodic elections, the more elective public offices there are, and the fewer appointive, the more responsible government would be. This line of reasoning was widely accepted and resulted in the establishment of systems of elective administrative positions at the statewide level. Thus, in New York, the Constitutional Convention of 1846 provided for the election of the hitherto appointive positions of: secretary of state, comptroller, treasurer, engineer and surveyor, three inspectors of prisons, and three canal commissioners. Together with the governor and the lieutenant governor, it brought to 13 the number of statewide elective officials. While this was later hailed, in language the proponents of the Jacksonian dogma would have applauded, as marking ". . . an epoch in the constitutional history of the state; for the first time the various branches of government were brought into more direct relation to the people than ever before . . ."[31] its effect on the power of the governor was devastating. Power in the executive became diffused. The governor could not act or speak on behalf of the executive branch, nor direct or coordinate its activities, for there were other power holders and wielders who acted out of their own interests. This is what de Tocqueville meant when, in an assessment of the executive power in the states in this period, he observed:

> The executive power is *represented* by the governor. It is not by accident that I have used this word; the governor *represents* this power, although he enjoys but a portion of its rights.[32]

Thus, the gains made by the governor in this period, with respect to his former position of subservience to the legislature, were balanced by the fact that the executive branch was severely weakened by internal division. And, while the emancipation from legislative domination was a significant step in the development of the governorship, these internal divisions were serious enough in their effect to lead students of government to assess the position of the governor at the mid-century mark as one of "innocuous desuetude"[33] and of the governor himself as a "chief executive in name only."[34]

1850-1915

The internal divisions suffered by the executive branch in the first half of the nineteenth century grew increasingly worse in the second half. While there were some gains in the governor's appointing power in states such as New York,[35] this period witnessed the growth, in most states, of a tremendous body of state administrative machinery independent of the governor. Moreover, the consequences of the diffusion of power in the executive became far more serious in this period than they were in earlier years.

The post Civil War years were a time of rapid economic growth and social change. The large scale expansion of such industries as banking, insurance, and the railroads led to the need for some forms of government regulation. The advent of the Industrial Age, with its social effects, led to an increased concern with such problems as the protection of public health and the care of dependents and delinquents by charities and correctional facilities. State legislatures were now confronted with whole new areas in which they had to set standards. The new legislation needed, of course, to be referred to some administrative body for enforcement; and the legislatures were faced with the choice of either referring the new laws to existing agencies or creating new ones expressly for this purpose. They chose the latter route for a variety of reasons.[36] One simple reason is that they were concerned with providing these administrative units with a sense of freshness and vitality lacking in the existing machinery. Another is that special interests, especially professions such as medicine and dentistry, agitated for the creation of agencies whose exclusive function it would be to work on matters of concern to those interests. The 1915 report of the Illinois Efficiency and Economy Committee observed that:

> For nearly every interest, however unimportant and, however closely related it may be in its nature to some other interest, a separate board has been created, each having its own staff of officials and employees, its own separate offices and its own administrative machinery.[37]

A third reason is the fact that new administrative agencies provided increased patronage for the members of the legislature; patronage, it should be pointed out, of a valuable sort. Governor Frank Lowden of Illinois pointed out two attractive features of appointment to such agencies:

> . . . [they] provided good places for aspirants to office, and, being a law unto itself, the members could attend to their private affairs and give one or two days a month—usually about the time the payrolls were made up—to the public service.[38]

Lastly, and most importantly, there was the traditional fear of concentrating power. In what Lipson refers to as the "reductio ad absurdum of the old theory of checks and balances,"[39] it was felt that here too, the more power was divided and shared, the safer the people were:

> The separation of powers had been first applied between the three major branches of government. Later, it was given a special application to the executive, and the chief executive power was diffused. Now, as the last stage, the lesser administrative activities were subdivided among numerous agencies, co-ordinate with each other. Each had its own statutory authorization from the legislature; each was a petty lord in its carefully delimited domain.[40]

The new administrative units were created in the form of boards and commissions,[41] and once established, they multiplied rapidly. Massachusetts was one of the first states to go the board and commission route.[42] Beginning with a state board of education in 1837, she added steadily to that, until, by the turn of the century, Massachusetts would have more than 200 such units,[43] or more than any other state.[44] New York, which in 1800 had total of 10 state agencies of all kinds and had only doubled this number by mid-century, had accumulated 81 separate departments, boards, and commissions[45] by 1900, and 169 by 1914—of which 108 were boards, and commissions.[46] In the early years of the twentieth century, every state had a minimum of 25 boards and commissions,[47] with the larger states, and some of the smaller, numbering about 100 or more.[48] Small wonder that turn of the century students of government characterized the board and commission as "the chief distinguishing characteristic of modern state administration."[49] One explanation for the great numbers of boards and commissions is that they were created for every conceivable purpose. James Q. Dealey, writing in 1905, testified that: "Every new line of activity results in the formation of a special board or commission until these can be counted by the score in almost every state."[50] Another explanation is the fact that once established, boards and commissions were difficult to dissolve. Governor Lowden explained this phenomenon succinctly: "There is nothing more difficult in government than to get rid of a lucrative office once established."[51] One major result of this rage to create new boards and commissions and extreme reluctance to abolish them, was that there arose many situations in which numbers of boards and commissions, created at different times, worked separately in related functional areas, with little regard being paid the resulting duplication and waste. New York affords a good example of this. In 1880, New York established a game and fish protectors agency; then, in 1885, it established a forest commission; in 1892, a commission of fisheries; in 1895, a forest, fish and game commission; and in 1897, a forest purchasing board.[52] By the time all the independent agencies were finally consolidated into one Conservation Department in 1926, they numbered 22. This is an entirely representative example of the situation in other areas in New York, and in other states.

The rise of the board and commission increased the fragmentation and lack of unity in the executive branch. While, to be sure, the governor's appointing power was increased as the legislature granted him a role in naming the membership of many boards and commissions, it was in all cases made clear that the boards and commissions were independent units and not extensions of his administrative arm. This was accomplished by denying the governor the power of removal and by establishing the terms of board and commission members in such a way as not to be coterminous with that of the governor. Combined with the continuation of the system of election of constitutional administrative officers other than the governor, the system of boards and commissions made for a greater diffusion of power in the executive branch than ever before. Woodrow Wilson, observing this situation in 1889, concluded that: "the governor . . . is not the 'Executive'; he is but a single piece of the executive. There are other pieces coordinated with him over which he has no direct official control."[53] Surveying the same scene Frank J. Goodnow offered this assessment:

> The governor is not the head of the administration in the commonwealth of the American union. American administrative law has added to the famous trinity of Montesquieu a fourth department, *viz*, the administrative department, which is almost entirely independent of the chief executive and which, as far as the central administration is concerned, is assigned to a number of officers not only independent of the governor but also independent of each other.[54]

More than its unprecedented scale, though, what distinguished the diffusion of power in the executive in the late nineteenth and early twentieth centuries from this diffusion in earlier periods was the fact that it had become a serious problem for the first time. The rapidly changing socioeconomic landscape, to which the state's partial and spontaneous response had been the creation of boards and commissions, made it imperative for government to offer effective leadership. Lipson quotes Lord Bryce's explanation, offered in the 1880s, for the states' ability to "rub along" with a system of fragmented administrative machinery: "The executive has little to do and comparatively small sums to handle," and adds that in fact

> A trend of affairs had already started before the 1880s which soon outdated this opinion. . . . The resources of the country were being exploited, and the industrial age with its attendant railways and factories was producing a new social environment and necessitating new social standards. The colliding and jostling of individualistic enterprise created a melange with which only the organized authority of government could cope. Government was at last called upon to govern.[55]

No longer was there "little to do." Nor were the sums small anymore. The increase in state expenditures was especially dramatic at the beginning of the twentieth century. In the 10-year period from 1903 to 1913, expenditures of the states more than doubled.[56] In New York, total expenditures over the 10 years 1896-1905 amounted to $258,460,052; while over the period 1906-1915 they came to $673,462,496.[57] From the year 1901, when expenditures came to $24,597,841, to 1915, when they were $94,902,371, New York experienced a 286 percent increase.[58]

Now that "government was at last called upon to govern," it was to the executive branch generally, and the governor in particular, that many people looked. One reason for this was that the early popular suspicion of the legislatures had, by now, grown to contempt. They were commonly perceived to be groups of timid, parochial, ignorant, and corrupt men. Of all these characteristics, wrote Bryce:

> Nothing is more remarkable about these state legislators than their timidity. No one seems to think of having an opinion of his own. In matters which touch the interests of his constituents, a member is, of course, their humble servant. In burning party questions—they are few and mostly personal—he goes with his party. In questions of general public policy he looks to see how the cat jumps.[59]

As a result, ". . . the meeting of the legislature is looked forward to with anxiety by the 'good citizens' . . . and its departure hailed as a deliverance."[60] New York's legislature, which he categorized "among the worst"[61] was described by Bryce as ". . . a Witche's (sic) Sabbath of jobbing, bribing, thieving, and prostitution of legislative power such as the world has seldom seen."[62] Of the Assembly specifically he wrote: "The Assembly includes many honest men, and a few rich men who do not need a doceur but the proportion of tainted men is large enough to pollute the whole lump."[63] This did not go unrecognized by the people. The New York Constitutional Convention of 1846 prohibited the legislature from granting divorces, authorizing lotteries, giving special charters to banks, and forming corporations by special, as opposed to general, acts—all great sources of corruption. The Constitutional Convention of 1894 placed further restrictions on the legislature's authority to grant exclusive privileges to particular corporations, and required all proposed legislation to be printed three days before it was voted upon. These restrictions were representative of the checks placed on the legislatures of other states—one popular check used by many states was the restriction of the legislative session to a mere 40 to 60 days, assuming that the less time the legislature sat, the less opportunity it would have to cause mischief.[64] The low status of the legislatures served to enhance the status of the governor, as Bryce noted:

> The decline . . . in the respect and confidence felt for and in the legislature has latterly, in some states, tended to attach more influence to the office of Governor, and has opened to a strong and upright man, the opportunity of making it a post of effective leadership. The people are coming to look upon the head of their commonwealth as the person responsible for giving them a firm and honest leadership.[65]

Another reason people looked to the governor for leadership was because the governorship had, in fact, become an effective position in certain areas in this period. This was especially true of the governor's legislative role, in which his greatest asset was his veto. In 1844, New Jersey ushered in a new era in the veto power by granting the governor an item veto on appropriation bills. Numbers of states followed suit, beginning with the southern states and eventually extending to other parts of the country—New York adopted such a veto in 1874. The veto power was also enhanced by the adoption of a change in the manner in which vetoes could be overruled. Traditionally, it was a majority of the legislators in attendance that was required to overrule a veto, thus making it possible for vetoes to be overruled with less than a majority of the full legislature. In 1873, Pennsylvania, followed a year later by

New York and soon therafter by other states, changed this requirement to a majority of the whole number of legislators. Thus fortified, the veto became an effective and vigorously used tool in the post Civil War period.[66] Another of the governor's legislative tools was his power, and duty, to communicate with the legislature, both to convey the general condition of the state and to make specific legislative recommendations. There the position of the governor as the representative of the state as a whole, as opposed to the localism of the legislators, was especially evident and effective.[67] Rounding out his power regarding legislation were the powers generally granted the governor to call extra sessions of the legislature and to adjourn it in the event the two houses disagreed on a time for adjournment. When one adds to the governor's well developed legislative role his traditional military powers consisting of the command of the state militia and his power to grant pardons and reprieves, it is evident that his powers in areas outside of administration were quite formidable. It was not surprising, therefore, that people would look to the governor for effective leadership in all areas.

But the governor could not offer it. Far from it, he was not even master of his own house. The typical late nineteenth and early twentieth century state executive branch was a diffused, uncoordinated mass of departments, boards, and commissions whose typical features were duplication and waste. Abernathy describes it this way:

> The typical state executive department . . . was multi-headed, with no unity of command or centralized control over the state's administrative structure. State constitutions listed not the governor alone, but five, six, seven, or more of the most important state officers as comprising the state executive department in which the executive power of the state was vested, and among whom it was divided. Both the state constitution and the legislature, in providing for the administrative agencies of the state, introduced a whole series of devices for breaking up and distributing authority. There was great variety in methods of appointment, terms of office were of varying lengths and frequently overlapped in the same agency, methods of removal varied where they were provided at all, officials of equal importance were elected and appointed, responsibility for the performance of related functions was diffused and assigned to several agencies. If there was any plan to the typical state administrative organization, it would appear to have been a planned planlessness, a conscious attempt at decentralization and disorganization designed to prevent concentrated authority at any point in state government.[68]

New York's "planned planlessness" was as bad as any. The constitution of 1894 declared that "the executive power shall be vested in a governor,"[69] but it provided for the election, and thus the independence from the governor, of the comptroller, attorney general, treasurer, secretary of state, and engineer and surveyor. The governor's power of appointment, albeit increased from what it was—in 1914 the number of officers he could appoint was 558[70]— was inhibited not only by the fact that the terms of administrative officers were often not coterminous with his, and that removal power was often not his, but also by the fact that it existed alongside fully 15 other methods of appointment.[71] There were, by 1914, 169 separate state agencies. These were uncoordinated and frequently overlapped in their jurisdictions. The following are but a few examples of this:[72] six commissions, 40 boards, and four departments held some degree of supervision over state institutions for defectives, delinquents, and dependents; 51 separate agencies shared the control of the parks, reservations, historical buildings, and monuments of the state; inspection and regulation of the preparation and sale of different food products was conducted separately by the Departments of Health, Agriculture and Labor; assessment, collection, and audit of taxes were carried out by the state controller's office as well as by the secretary of state, Excise Department and tax commission; in the field of education, there were two schools of forestry, two schools of veterinary, and nine secondary schools of agriculture operated by the state, all of whom had little or nothing to do with each other; in the area of laboratory research, three agencies, the Health and Agriculture Departments and the hospital commission, operated laboratories for testing food stuffs, and two, the Highway and Education Departments, operated laboratories for the testing of rocks and stones, all of which were run independently of each other. These examples were representative of the situation throughout the executive branch.

Such was the state of the executive when "at last called upon to govern." If the governor was to respond to this call, it was obvious that some kind of reorganization was essential. There were some who were already working toward such a reorganization.

THE STATE REORGANIZATION MOVEMENT

The problems of state government were not the subject of extensive study in the eighteenth and nineteenth centuries.[73] Bryce observed that state government was

> . . . the part of the American political system which received least attention both from foreign and from native writers . . . the character, power, and working of the states as separate self-governing bodies received little attention or illustration.[74]

Reformers and reorganizers, too, focused their attention on the national and local governments before turning to the states.[75] When the seriousness of the problems of state government administration became increasingly apparent in the first few years of the nineteenth century, thinkers and writers on American governmental institutions turned their attention to the states. Many agreed with Walter F. Dodd, an early writer on state government and reorganization, that Bryce's assessment in the 1880s that "the government of the cities is the one conspicuous failure of the United States," was no longer valid by the early 1900s and that the state governments had replaced those of the cities as the most serious problem area.[76] The first decade and a half of the nineteenth century saw numbers of books and a rash of articles in such publications as the *American Political Science Review*, the *Annals of the American Academy of Political and Social Science*, the *Political Science Quarterly*, and, occasionally, in the *New Republic*, *North American Review*, *Outlook*, and the *Atlantic*, among others, treating some or all aspects of the problems of state government and its reorganization. While it is not altogether clear that Herbert Croly's 1911 observation that:

> Among the many serious political and economic problems with which the American democracy is confronted, there is none, in respect to which public opinion is more profoundly interested and more radically divided than in those connected with state political reorganization.[77]

was an accurate appraisal of the degree of public interest in state government and its reform, it is safe to say that it applied to people concerned with the problems of government; and that the concern displayed by them helped make the public at large more aware of the issue than they had previously been.

The early writers stressed first and foremost the need to eliminate the ineconomy and inefficiency of the fragmented state administrative systems and replace them with a structure which would ensure "economy and efficiency." Just what they meant by the phrase "economy and efficiency" has, of course, been the subject of much debate and discussion among students of the reorganization movement.[78] One interpretation submits that "economy" referred to a general reduction of state expenditures, while "efficiency" referred to the elimination of waste in administration. Another defines "efficiency" as the effective provision of services to those in need of those services and believes that it was "economy" which referred to the elimination of waste. In fact, both interpretations are correct as different reorganization theorists adopted one or the other and as the reorganization movement in different places and at different times used the phrase in the sense it found most appropriate.[79] However they were meant, "economy and efficiency" were not the only concerns of the reorganization writers.[80] They were also concerned with an issue of more profound concern to democratic government—the responsibility of government to the governed.

Diffusion in administration, the reorganization theorists argued, meant diffusion in responsibility; and that, they submitted, was a contradiction in terms. For a system in which large numbers of people shared authority in identical areas, was a system in which no one person was answerable for the activities, or inactivity, in those areas. Albert Stickney formulated it his way:

> The responsibility of more men than one, even with small numbers, is worth little. The responsibility of men in large numbers is worth nothing. . . . We lay it down as a universal political law, that the division of power means the division of responsibility; and the division of responsibility means its destruction.[81]

It was ironic that the champions of divided power, whose motivation lay in the prevention of what they saw as the inevitable abuses resulting from concentrated power (or, simply put, ensuring government's responsibility to the people), should now themselves be charged with having created a system whose irresponsibility was built-in and assured.

The attack, however, was not on their motives, which none sought to impugn; it was on the overapplication of a theory whose aims were admirable but whose value was questionable. The attackers of the system of divided power did not share the assumptions of its creators regarding power and its concentration. Not that they were unaware of the possibilities for the abuse of power, but rather because they were at least equally sensitive to the possibilities for its constructive use. They appreciated the fears of the early constitution framers and argued that the governments they constructed were less expressions of how government could act as a positive force than reactions to their experience with Great Britain.

> Political institutions in America have been designed on the principle of distrust. *Fear* of the people, *fear* of the legislature, *fear* of the executive, have inspired constitution makers from the very beginning, . . .[82]

observed Frederic C. Howe, and it was this "political science of negation"[83] which motivated the framers. Separation of powers, which lay at the core of the systems they framed, was an obstacle to governments acting effectively; and when extended, as it was in the prevailing state governments, it made for irresponsible government. In attacking the separation of powers philosophy, these writers were, of course, continuing a tradition begun by earlier scholars—most recently, towards the end of the nineteenth century, carried on by Gamaliel Bradford and Woodrow Wilson.[84] In fact, their general argument had substantially been made over a century ago in the prescient observation of the perceptive French statesman Turgot on the first state constitutions, in 1778:

> I see in the greatest number an unreasonable imitation of the usages of England. Instead of bringing all the authorities into one, . . . they have established different bodies. A house of representatives, a council, a governor, because England has a House of Commons, Lords, and a King. They undertake to balance these different authorities as if the same equilibrium of power which has been thought necessary to balance the enormous preponderance of royalty could be of any use in Republics, formed upon the equality of all citizens, and as if every article which constitutes different bodies was not a source of divisions. By striving to escape imaginary dangers they have created real ones.[85]

The reorganization theorists did not advocate the absolute concentration of all governmental authority as did Turgot, but they did argue that the ineconomy, inefficiency, and irresponsibility of the divided state administrative systems confirmed that the dangers of division were indeed real.

Administrative authority and responsibility should be concentrated in the governor, argued the reorganization writers. In making their case, they constantly referred to what they considered two analogous situations.[86] Following the lead of Woodrow Wilson whose 1887 essay declared that "the field of administration is a field of business,"[87] they argued that the organizational structure of business corporations provided a useful model for the administration of government. The structure of most corporations consisted of a president, who was its chief operating officer, and a board of directors to whom the president was responsible. The president was given free reign in appointing officers of his choice to head the various divisions of the corporation and in directing its daily affairs. Ultimately he was answerable to the board which could dismiss him, but until it did, his authority was unquestioned. Evidently the private sector was satisfied with this arrangement; was it unreasonable to assume it would serve the public sector equally well? The reorganizers believed in this analogy, but more than that, they recognized its appeal to the business community. Charles Beard acknowledged this:

> . . . for the purpose of discussing anew the fundamentals of govern-
> ment with lawyers and businessmen . . . an appeal to their experi-
> ences with corporation organization and practices touches a more
> tender spot than the most ingenious references to the experiences of
> European countries in their efforts to establish responsible govern-
> ment. . . . There are tactics as well as wisdom in seeking principles for
> the reconstruction of state government in institutional experience in
> its broadest sense—in public and private experience.[88]

To those who resisted the business-government analogy and were still uneasy over concentrations of power in government, they offered the example of the federal government. While there were problems in the national executive similar to those in the states', the President was far more the center of the executive branch than were the governors. His was the only elective office. Under him were a few main departments whose affairs he directed through their officers who were appointed and removable by him. And yet, despite this relative concentration of authority, the people were satisfied that the system performed responsibly; why should this not be the case at the state level?

Their general objective being the concentration of administrative authority and responsibility in the governor, the reorganizers sought three specific means to that end: consolidation of adminis-trative agencies; appointment by the governor of the main adminis-trative officers, as opposed to their election; and an executive budget. Consolidation of agencies entailed substituting a few large departments for the mass of offices, boards, and commissions. Each department would have a prescribed set of functions and all such functions would be placed under its exclusive jurisdiction. The departments would be placed under the direction of the governor and he would exercise this power of direction through the depart-ment heads who would be his appointees. On this second principle of gubernatorial appointment of department heads, rather than their election, the reorganizers received help from a different source.

Among the reform movements current in the early years of this century was the short ballot movement. While students of govern-ment had long decried the state and city electoral systems which required citizens to vote for candidates to so huge a number of offices that the voters couldn't possibly know much about most of them, it was not until the first decade of the twentieth century that the issue gained wide public attention. In large measure, this was due to the efforts of one man, Richard S. Childs. Childs was a serious student of government and a concerned citizen, but, most of all, he was a masterful publicist. His writings on the short ballot were not learned treatises on political theory but collections of brief, punchy arguments offered in language the layman could understand. They often included catchy slogans and phrases— indeed, the phrase "short ballot" was first introduced by Childs in his well known 1909 essay of the same name in the *Outlook*.[89] More than anything else, it was Childs' tactics of appealing to the voters in terms they could understand that made the short ballot issue the subject of popular concern in this period.

The short ballot advocates believed that the most effective way to convince the public that the long ballot made a mockery of the electoral system and was essentially undemocratic, was to point out to the only vaguely aware voters just how many offices they were being asked to fill regularly. In New York City, they pointed out, 500 separate state, county, and city offices were filled by election in every four-year cycle.[90] In addition, for those who participated in party elections, they could expect, in a four-year cycle, to vote for members of the following committees: city, county, and assembly district; and delegates to the following conventions: city, county, borough, judicial district, congressional district, senatorial district, assembly district, aldermanic district, and municipal court district.[91] The Democratic primary ballot for the thirty-second Assembly District was eight and a half inches by two feet four inches and contained 835 candidates.[92] Who could pretend that the voters were familiar with even a good number of the candidates in these contests and voted on the basis of their relative merits. And who could argue that such a system benefited anyone but the entrenched party machines who ran their handpicked slates, secure in the knowledge that the party faithful would vote them in with no questions asked beyond party or organizational affiliation. Last, and worst of all, who could deny that, once elected, the parties' designees, having won office solely by virtue of their organizational affiliation, would be beholden to their benefactors, the bosses, and perform according to their dictates. Thus, concluded the short ballot advocates, the long ballot assured government not by the people, but by the party bosses; or, as the movement referred to them, the "invisible government," "unpopular government," or "government by experts."

Because their emphasis was on the ballot and democratic government, there were those in the short ballot movement who did not realize that their objective, the reduction of the number of elective offices, was identical to that of the reorganizers. Beard pointed this out:

> . . . independent of the question as to the capacity of the voters to
> select and control a vast horde of officers, the proper grouping of

related functions and their subordination to responsible heads will automatically produce the short ballot. . . . This is not commonly taken into account by those short ballot advocates who view the question from the standpoint of the voters.[93]

Beard was one short ballot advocate who did recognize that the cause of the movement and that of the reorganization movement was essentially a common one. In fact, in their attack on the "invisible government" of the unseen, but powerful bosses, the short ballot advocates shared a common enemy with the reorganizers. The reorganization movement, too, complained of the grip the bosses held over the machinery of government and argued that the prevailing state administrative systems fostered the health and growth of "invisible government." This point was made by many of the reorganizers, among them, Walker D. Hines:

> The political boss is an ever-present meance in American politics. Could any system develop him more completely than our system of divided responsibility? Can there be any place where the "invisible government" of the boss can succeed to a greater extent than in a form of government where it is almost impossible to locate any visible signs of responsibility?[94]

Thus, the reorganization and short ballot movements, by virtue of both their immediate objectives and a prime object of their attacks, were ideal allies. For a practical matter, whether those in the movement realized it or not—and most, like Beard, did—the short ballot movement ". . . initiated to strengthen popular control of government and to relieve the voter of an impossible civic task, was discovered to play directly into the hands of the advocates of unity and responsibility in administration.[95]

The third objective of the reorganizers went beyond structural reorganization. Little thought was given before the turn of the century to the need for a budget system in the states. Expenditures were not great and revenues were sufficient to meet what expenditures there were. The increased demands on government services at the turn of the century and the discontinuance at this time of the general property tax—then the major source of state revenue[96]—in response to the pressures of local governments intent on using it as their own revenue source, combined to bring serious financial pressure on the states for the first time. As taxes rose, taxpayers associations and chambers of commerce began demanding economies, both in the sense of reducing overall expenditures and eliminating waste in administration. To this end, they urged adoption of a vehicle they believed would help ensure economy, a budget system. It was immediately apparent, however, that the structure of the state governments was ill suited to the coordination required in a budget system. Appropriations were made on the basis of separate requests made to the legislature by the many separate administrative agencies. There was no coordination between these agency requests, nor did anyone have the authority to undertake any such coordination. In addition, there were several elected state officers who possessed some degree of fiscal authority. If, as they believed, "an Integrated Administrative System [was] the Essential Basis of a Proper Budget System,"[97] wholesale changes in the prevailing state administrative structures were imperative. In this way, many citizens whose primary concern was reducing their tax burdens were drawn to the objectives of the reorganization movement. The reorganizers welcomed this support, but, beyond this, they too were interested in the adoption of an executive budget. An executive budget, with its integration, coordination, and emphasis on the central role of the chief executive officer, was consonant with their goal of consolidating administrative authority and responsibility and of making the governor the hub of the administrative system. The executive budget complemented and reinforced the objectives of agency consolidation and a short ballot.

PROGRESS OF THE REORGANIZATION MOVEMENT TO 1915

Little progress was made by the reorganization movement in the pre-1915 period. The movement was a small one in those early years, consisting almost exclusively of concerned scholars and a relatively few civic minded individuals. They received scant support from people in state government and the public at large. Most legislators and government bureaucrats perceived that implementation of the reorganizers' plan would result in a reduction of their own power, while the public at large was simply not yet educated to the need for reorganization. Moreover, the changes envisioned by the reorganizers seemed to contradict the traditional verities regarding concentrated authority and the sanctity of the ballot box. All this ensured that the reception accorded the reorganization advocates would be a hostile one. Beard described this reception:

> Mr. Croly, with his program of simplification and responsibility in government, the short ballot advocates, and all other reconstructionists were simply ruled out of court. They were attempting to lay profane hands on the Ark of the Convenant. They were met with shrill cries about the gods, the sacred oracles, the Elysian fields, the fathers and the separation of powers. . . . from Montana or Wyoming

came the solemn warning . . . that the executive appointment of the state veterinarian smacked of monarchy.[98]

Such opposition, it must be said, was not unexpected by the reorganizers. For though they were confident of their eventual success, they had no illusions concerning the difficulty of their task. Croly, referring to one aspect of reorganization, wrote in 1911 that:

> The prediction may be confidently advanced that eventually the need of consolidation in our own state political institutions will have to be faced. But the attempt to meet it will probably make very slow headway. An American electorate usually jumps at the opportunity of casting more votes, but it is loth to believe that more votes do not mean more power or to surrender any vote, which it has once obtained.[99]

John M. Mathews, writing of the need to educate the public on the necessity for reorganization, cautioned that:

> The development of such an educated public opinion in favor of radical changes in state government is a slow process, because it is necessary for the people to rid themselves of some venerable ideas and traditional notions. . . .[100]

Thus, the reorganization advocates were realistic about the chances for rapid reorganization, and it was this realism that caused them not to despair when their efforts did not meet with immediate success.

Some progress was made in the early part of the second decade of the century when the movement gained important allies in the form of the newly created state commissions on economy and efficiency. These commissions were created in the wake of President Taft's national Commission on Economy and Efficiency. That commission carried out its investigations from 1910 to 1913 and issued a series of reports dealing with the poor organization of the national executive and the need for a national budget. While the commission's recommendations received little attention from Congress, its reports were widely read and suggested to many people the need for examination of the state executive branches as well. Wisconsin acted first, establishing a board of public affairs in 1911 which would serve a function similar to that of the national commission on the state level. In 1912, New Jersey and Massachusetts established state commissions on economy and efficiency, and in 1913, Illinois, New York, Pennsylvania, Iowa, and South Dakota established similar commissions. Between 1911 and 1919, commissions or committees aimed at promoting efficiency and economy were created by 27 states.[101] The commissions almost invariably backed the reforms advocated by the reorganizers and were a valuable addition to the movement. For the first time, the movement was given a voice by an institutional part of the state governments.

The establishment of the state economy and efficiency commissions and their support of the reorganization movement, important developments as they were, did not, however, represent a new, popular acceptance of the need for reorganization. State legislators and bureaucrats still felt threatened by the reforms advocated by the movement, and the great majority of the electorate still was unconvinced of the need for reorganization. The struggle was just beginning.

THE PRE-1915 REORGANIZATION MOVEMENT IN NEW YORK

As in the overall reorganization movement, there is little to report of the progress of the movement in New York in the pre-1915 period. Nevertheless, it is true that the early struggle for reorganization fared better in New York than in most other states. In good measure, this was due to the identification with the movement of that state's widely respected governor, Charles Evans Hughes. Indeed, the beginning of the fight for reorganization in New York has been dated as 1906, one year before Hughes' ascension to the governorship and the year in which he committed himself publicly to reorganization.[102] While Luther Gulick's observation that ". . . Charles Evans Hughes was the first Governor to rethink the problem of the organization of the executive in order to make that executive really responsible and effective"[103] is presumably subject to qualifications—there had, in fact, been several New York governors who preceded Hughes in giving thought and expression to this problem[104]—it was Hughes who made the issue a constant and outstanding theme of his administrations. Perhaps nowhere better did he articulate this theme than in his 1909 inaugural address:

> While the governor represents the highest power in the state, there is frequently observed a popular misapprehension as to its scope. There is a wide domain of executive or administrative action over which he has no control, or slight control. There are several elected state officers, not accountable to the governor, who exercise within their prescribed spheres most important executive powers. . . . The multiplication of executive duties incident to the vast and necessary increase in state activities has resulted in the creation of a large number of departments exercising administrative powers of first consequence to the people. The governor has the power of appointment but in most cases the concurrence of the senate is necessary. The terms of these officers are generally longer than the governor's

term. And in their creation the legislature with few exceptions had reserved final administrative control to the senate in making the heads of departments, to whose appointment the senate's consent is necessary, removable only by it. . . . A division of accountability which practically results in no real accountability to anyone lessens the proper stimulus to efficiency. . . . Responsibility to the people is the essential safeguard of free institutions. This does not mean the election of all or even a greater number of administrative officers, for undue burdens upon the electoral machine would defeat its purpose. But it would seem to imply that distribution of administrative powers should have as its correlative the proper centralization of responsibility. It may fairly be said to require that the executive authority, exercising the appointment power under whatever check, should be responsible for administration and should have the control upon which such responsibility must rest.[105]

Hughes' outspoken support of reorganization, though unsuccessful in actually bringing about any reorganization during his administrations—reorganization measures were introduced in the legislature in the 1909 and 1910 sessions and were defeated by overwhelming majorities—did influence many people's attitudes regarding reorganization, especially within his own Republican party. The party's 1910 gubernatorial candidate, Henry L. Stimson, gave a short ballot high priority throughout his campaign, and its 1912 platform committed the party to one.

If, as has been suggested, the struggle for reorganization in New York dates from the time Hughes threw his support behind the movement, thereby helping it to be taken seriously by many who otherwise would not, the first real movement towards actual reorganization was taken by Governor William Sulzer early in 1913. Inspired, no doubt, by the work of the Taft Commission and the growing number of state economy and efficiency commissions, Sulzer appointed a three-man Committee of Inquiry to conduct investigations into the expenditures of the state. On March 21 of that year, the committee submitted a report to the governor analyzing state appropriations for the current year as well as agency requests for the following year, and recommending the reduction of a number of the agency estimates. It also recommended the establishment of a permanent state board of estimate which would review agency requests and formulate a comprehensive appropriations bill; and a permanent Department of Efficiency and Economy, to be headed by a commissioner of efficiency and economy, who would be authorized to carry out investigations of state administrative services and make recommendations with a view to upgrading their economy and efficiency. The committee's recommendations were accepted by the legislature and the two suggested bodies were established later that year, with the provision that the commissioner of efficiency and economy also function as the secretary of the board of estimate. In addition to the efficiency and economy commissioner, the board of estimate included the governor, lieutenant governor, president of the Senate, speaker of the Assembly, chairman of the Senate finance committee, chairman of the Assembly ways and means committee, comptroller, and attorney general. All executive agencies were required to file appropriations requests for the ensuing fiscal year with the board. These requests were reviewed by the board, which would then proceed to formulate a comprehensive state budget. The board's budget would also include statements on the amount required to meet the debt service, estimated revenues, and unexpended balances of the state. This centralized and comprehensive arrangement was a revolutionary one and prompted a contemporary scholar to declare that it ". . . places the state in the lead in budgetary reform."[106] The Department of Efficiency and Economy consisted of the following divisions and bureaus: general administration division; bureau of finance and budget; bureau of curative, charitable, and penal institutions; bureau of public works department; bureau of miscellaneous departments; and an advisory board. The mandate of the department was broad, authorizing it to conduct investigations throughout the executive branch and to make appropriate recommendations. In a very short time the department became, as did most similar bodies in other states, a staunch supporter of reorganization—the substance of which support will be treated later.

Another positive development in this period was the progress made by the short ballot movement. Richard Childs was not only a superlative propagandist, but an able organizer as well. In 1909, Childs founded a National Short Ballot Organization and added a separate New York organization the following year. He enlisted the participation of eminent public figures as officers, the most notable of whom, in the national organization, was Woodrow Wilson, and, through the mails, urged people to join as "short ballot advocates." Childs' appeal struck a responsive chord and the number of "advocates" swelled.[107] By 1912, support for a short ballot found its way into the Republican and Progressive parties' platforms, and in 1914 the Democrats added their support. In contrast to the meager response to a short ballot measure introduced in the Assembly in 1909—only twenty-six members supported the measure—a short ballot was actually passed by the Assembly in 1914.

These were the only developments of note in this early period of the struggle for reorganization in New York. While there was some movement toward the aims of the reorganizers, principally in the area of a short ballot and, to a lesser extent, an executive budget, none of their objectives were actually realized—the short ballot came closest when the Assembly voted for one in 1914 but the Senate failed to follow suit. Moreover, the year 1915 held major setbacks for the movement in the form of the legislature's abolition of both the board of estimate and the Efficiency and Economy Department, actions taken largely for political reasons unrelated to the reorganization issue but harmful, nonetheless, to the cause of reorganization. In sum, the pre-1915 reorganization movement in New York, although accorded a better popular reception than elsewhere, was also in its beginning stage.

NOTES

[1]William H. Young, "The Development of the Governorship," *State Government* 31 (Summer 1958): 183.

[2]Arthur W. Bromage, *State Government and Administration in the United States* (New York: Harper and Bros., 1936), p. 165. Bromage did not include the early colonial stage or the period in which most of the governors were "detested minions of Royal power." Nor is it necessary for our purposes to focus on this period here.

[3]Quoted in Leslie Lipson, *The American Governor from Figurehead to Leader* (Chicago: University of Chicago Press, 1939), p. 7.

[4]Allan Nevins, *The American States During and After the Revolution 1775-1789* (New York: The MacMillan Co., 1924), p. 166.

[5]Partially the result of its conservative authorship—the document was largely the work of Robert Livingstone, Gouverneur Morris, and John Jay—and partially, in Charles C. Thatch's view, because it was framed late (in 1777) and had the benefit of the experience of the state constitutions which preceded it, all of which provided for a weak executive with unhappy results (Charles C. Thatch, *The Creation of the Presidency 1775-1789* [Baltimore: The Johns Hopkins University Press, 1923: 2nd printing, 1969], p. 34).

[6]Lipson, p. 13.

[7]Nevins, p. 9.

[8]The officers whose manner of appointment was prescribed by the constitution included the following: the governor and lieutenant governor—elected by the people; state treasurer—elected by the legislature; subordinate judicial officers, such as clerks and attorneys—appointed by the courts in which they served; and town officials—elected by the people.

[9]One exception was New York, in which the people voted for governor, serving to underscore the relative strength of that state's executive.

[10]James Madison, *Debates on the Adoption of the Federal Constitution*, ed. Jonathan Elliot, 5 vols. (Philadelphia: J. B. Lippincott & Co., 1859), 5:327. This quotation and others by Madison and Jefferson which follow are classic observations on the status of the early governors and legislatures and are frequently cited in the literature on the development of the governorship.

[11]Idem, *The Federalist*, ed. Jacob E. Cooke (New York: Meridian Books, The World Publishing Co., 1961), p. 324.

[12]Thomas Jefferson, *Notes on the State of Virginia*, ed. William Peden (Philadelphia: Prichard and Hall, 1788; reprint ed., Chapel Hill: University of North Carolina, 1955), p. 120.

[13]Madison, *The Federalist*, p. 331.

[14]The turbulent conditions under which New York was forced to frame its constitution provide an extreme example of these pressures. The Provincial Congress, acting as a Constitutional Convention, initially met at White Plains and then, as the British advanced, was forced to adjourn to Harlem, Kingsbridge, Philipse Manor, Fishkill, Poughkeepsie, and, finally, to Kingston.

[15]New York Bureau of Municipal Research, "The Constitution and Government of the State of New York: An Appraisal," *Municipal Research*, no. 61 (May 1915), p. 57.

[16]Nevins, p. 166.

[17]Ibid., p. 171.

[18]Arthur N. Holcombe, *State Government in the United States* (New York: The MacMillan Co., 1916), p. 108.

[19]Ibid.

[20]It is commonly acknowledged that it was the strong New York governorship upon which the Presidency was modeled. Thatch wrote: "There is no need to cross the Atlantic to find a working model of the American Presidency. That it was the New York governorship is evident enough" (Thatch, p. 176).

[21]Bryon R. Abernathy, *Some Persisting Questions Concerning the Constitutional State Executive* (Lawrence, Kansas: The University of Kansas Publications, Governmental Research Series, no. 23, 1960), p. 3. Just how much of an influence it was is difficult to gauge. Lipson believes it established "a model which [the states] have been continually approaching" (Lipson, p. 17), while Holcombe wrote that it merely "accelerated the process" of revising the distribution of power in the state governments (Holcombe, p. 74).

[22]A full account of this intrigue and controversy can be found in J. M. Gitterman, "The Council of Appointment in New York," *Political Science Quarterly* 7 (March 1892): 80-115.

[23]Gitterman believed it was Jay's intention to have only the governor make nominations and that, for some reason, he failed to make this explicit (ibid., p. 90).

[24]These are the figures offered by Henry W. Hill (Henry W. Hill, *Development of Constitutional Law in New York State* [Buffalo: The Peter Paul Book Co., 1896], p. 19) and William C. Morey (William C. Morey, *The Government of New York, Its History and Administration* [New York: The MacMillan, Co., 1902], p. 46). Frank J. Goodnow, in making a point regarding the large number of appointive positions in this period, cited an 1821 schedule listing 7,000 civil and 8,000 military positions (Frank J. Goodnow, *Comparative Administrative Law*, 2 vols. [New York: G. P. Putnam's Sons, 1893], 1:77, n. 1).

[25]Quoted in John Ferguson, "Comparison and Growth of Administrative Powers of the Governors of New York and New Jersey" (Law Thesis, New York University, 1944), p. 11.

[26]The convention gave the power to appoint masters and examiners in chancery, certain military officers, and all judicial officers except justices of the peace, to the governor with the approval of the senate. The power to appoint the rest of the administrative and judicial officers was distributed between the legislature and the electorate.

[27]J. Hampden Dougherty, *Constitutional History of the State of New York*, 2nd ed. (New York: Neale, 1915), p. 111.

[28]Austin F. Macdonald, *American State Government and Administration* (New York: Thomas Y. Crowell, 1934), p. 23.

[29]Abernathy, p. 3.

[30]Bromage, p. 167.

[31]Morey, p. 49.

[32]Alexis de Tocqueville, *Democracy in America* 2 vols. (New York: Vintage Books, 1945), 1:88.

[33]Finla G. Crawford, *State Government* (New York: Henry Holt and Co., 1931),p. 162.

[34]Holcombe, p. 281.

[35]The first serious attempt to increase the governor's appointing power in this period came out of the Constitutional Convention of 1867. The constitution drafted by that convention proposed abolition of the independent positions of canal commissioner and superintendent of state prisons and the substitution for them of officers appointed by the governor. This constitution was defeated. A significant gain was made in 1872, when the recommendations of a legislative commission, giving the governor powers of appointment and removal, with approval of the senate, over the superintendent of state prisons and superintendent of public works, was approved by the legislature and subsequently added to the constitution in 1876. A more ambitious proposal by the commission that the governor be authorized to appoint the secretary of state, attorney general, and state engineer and surveyor, was defeated. The Constitutional Convention of 1894 added to the appointing power of the governor in providing for his appointments to the state board of charities, state commission in lunacy, and state commission of prisons. While these gains increased the governor's appointing power by the end of the century over what it had been at the time of the Constitutional Convention of 1846, when the only constitutional offices left within the governor's patronage were military, the governor's appointing power was not substantial, as Margaret C. Alexander explained:

"... If the development of the governor's constitutional power of appointment from the earliest constitution to date were presented graphically a very irregular line would result. From a median point of departure the line of growth would drop a number of degrees to indicate the amendment of 1801 which granted councilors concurrent power of nomination with the governor. In 1821 it would make a sharp rise and would follow along an elevated plateau until 1846 when it would drop almost to zero. In 1876 it would start to climb very gradually but the provisions of the constitution of 1894 would cause it to end at a point below the starting point of 1777" (Margaret C. Alexander, *The Development of the Power of the State Executive With Special Reference to the State of New York*, Smith College Studies in History, no. 3 [Northampton, MA: Smith College, 1917], p 181).

All this refers to the governor's power of appointment of constitutional officers and not of members of statutory bodies. With the rise of boards and commissions, which were statutory agencies—with the exception of the aforementioned board of charities, and commissions in lunacy and prisons—the governor's appointing power, as will be seen, gained measurably.

[36]See Lipson, pp. 25-29.

[37]Quoted in Lipson, p. 28.

[38]Frank O. Lowden, "Reorganizing the Administration of a State," *National Municipal Review* 15 (January 1926): 9.

[39]Lipson, p. 29.

[40]Ibid.

[41]The difference between a board and a commission is often not recognized and the terms are often mistakenly used interchangeably. In good measure, the confusion is due, as Austin F. Macdonald has pointed out, to the fact that legislatures frequently created a board and labelled it a commission and vice versa (Macdonald, p. 351). There is, in fact, a difference. Boards consist of groups of persons, often lay people, serving part time and leaving the day to day detail of their work to full time experts. Commissions consist of groups working full time at what, by virtue of their experience and training, they are expert in. The different kinds of boards and commissions were categorized as: industrial, scientific, supervisory, examining, educational, executive, and corrective and philanthropic (Francis H. White, "The Growth and Future of State Boards and Commissions," *Political Science Quarterly* 18 [December 1903]: 635-645).

[42]Holcombe, p. 286.

[43]Walter F. Dodd, *State Government* (New York: The Century Co., 1922), p. 244.

[44]White, p. 646.

[45]Crawford, p. 182.

[46]New York State Department of Efficiency and Economy, *Government of the State of New York: A Survey of Its Organization and Functions* (Albany: J. B. Lyon Co., Printers, 1915), p. vii, x.

[47]Charles H. Crennan, *A Survey of State Executive Organization and A Plan of Reorganization* (Menasha, Wisconsin: George Banta Publishing Co., 1916), p. 19.

[48]Examples are: Texas, "nearly one hundred" (Frank M. Stewart, "The Reorganization of State Administration in Texas," *University of Texas Bulletin* no. 2507 [Austin: University of Texas, 1925], p. 24); Pennsylvania, 139 (Crawford, p. 182); Michigan, 116; Maryland, 85; and Illinois and Delaware, "more than 100" (Dodd, p. 244).

[49]See Leonard A. Blue, "Recent Tendencies in State Administration," *The Annals of the American Academy of Political and Social Science* 18 (November 1901): 434; and Thomas H. Reed, *Government For the People* (New York: B. W. Huebsch, 1915), p. 182.

[50]James Q. Dealey, "Our State Constitutions," *The Annals* 30 (March 1907): 33. An example of the ludicrous lengths to which states went in creating boards and commissions is afforded by one instance in New Jersey. When the legislature decided to establish a state park on the site where Washington crossed the Delaware, it created the Washington Crossing Commission. Soon after, the legislature decided to especially attempt to preserve the rock upon which Washington is said to have stood surveying the river prior to crossing it—surely enough, a Washington Rock Commission was duly appointed! (John S. Pardee, "Government Running Wild," *The Outlook* 3 (November 10, 1915): 621.

[51]Lowden, p. 9.

[52]Lipson, pp. 29-30.

[53]Woodrow Wilson, *The State and Federal Governments* (Boston: D. C. Heath and Co., Publisher, 1889), p. 69.

[54]Goodnow, 1:136-137.

[55]Lipson, pp. 24-25.

[56]Holcombe, p. 308.

[57]John A. Hennessy, *What's the Matter With New York?* (New York: The O'Connell Press, 1916), p. 22.

[58]Ibid., p. 7. The magnitude of this increase is further dramatized by the fact that in this same period the increase in population was only 34.5 percent (ibid.).

[59]James Bryce, *The American Commonwealth*, 2nd ed., 2 vols. (New York: The Macmillan Co., 1912) 1:552.

[60]Ibid., 1:551.

[61]Ibid., 1:570.

[62]Ibid., 1:546.

[63]Ibid., 2:164. Concerning the New York Assembly, Bryce relates a story which he offers as representative of the way things worked:

> "A friend of mine who sat for some years in the New York Assembly was once importuned by an Irish member to support that particular member's little bill. He answered that he could not, because the bill was against the Constitution. 'Och, Mr. Robert,' was the reply, 'shure the Constitution should niver be allowed to come between friends'" (Ibid., 1:561).

[64]Frederick C. Howe, "The Constitution and Public Opinion," *Proceedings of the Academy of Political Science* 5 (New York, October 1914), p. 9. To be sure, there was another attraction to shortening the legislative session; legislators were commonly paid per session, and the shorter the session, the less the public would have to spend.

[65]Bryce, 1:501.

[66]For a discussion of the growth and use of the veto power in New York in this period, see Alexander, pp. 193-198.

[67]For a discussion of the growth and use of the governor's messages and recommendations to the legislature in New York in this period, see ibid., pp. 188-193.

[68]Abernathy, p. 5.

[69]New York, Constitution (1894), art. 4, ed. Francis N. Thorpe, The Federal and State Constitutions, 7 vols. (Washington: Government Printing Office, 1909) 5: 2709.

[70]Alexander, p. 188.

[71]New York Bureau of Municipal Research, pp. 36-37. There were also seven different methods of removal and suspension (ibid., pp. 40-41).

[72]See New York State Department of Efficiency and Economy, pp. vii-x.

[73]This is true even of works limited to one or several aspects of state government. General treatises on state government were not written at all until the 20th century. In 1911, Paul S. Reinsch published what is regarded as the "pioneer general source book" on state government, Readings on American State Government (Roy V. Peel, State Government Today [Albuquerque: University of New Mexico Press, 1948], p. 1), and in 1916, Arthur N. Holcombe published the first textbook, State Government in the United States.

[74]Bryce, 1:411-412. Franklin Jameson made the same observation regarding the paucity of written historical material on the states and their governments: "The most neglected field in American history is the field of state history—the constitutional and political history of the individual states" (Franklin J. Jameson, An Introduction to the Study of the Constitutional and Political History of the States, Johns Hopkins University Studies in Historical and Political Science, 4th series, no. 5 [Baltimore: John Murphy and Co., printers, 1886], p. 6).

[75]Dwight Waldo considers this a "valid generalization" despite the fact that there were some nineteenth century studies of centralization in state governments (Dwight Waldo, The Administrative State [New York: The Ronald Press Co., 1948], p. 34, n. 33).

[76]Walter F. Dodd, "Proposed Reforms in State Government Organization," American Political Science Review 5 (May 1910): 243.

[77]Herbert Croly, "State Political Reorganization," Proceedings of the American Political Science Association 8 (Buffalo, New York and Toronto, Ontario, Dec. 27-30, 1911): 122. Croly, an early and ardent champion of state government reorganization, was capable of exaggerating the degree of interest in reorganization, as he did its merits—in his classic, The Promise of American Life, Croly sings the praises of state government reorganization, suggesting, at one point, that, "In fact, a really regenerated state government might even consider the possible means of preventing crime and insanity" (Herbert Croly, The Promise of American Life [New York: The MacMillan Co., 1909; reprint ed., Cambridge, Mass.: Harvard University Press, 1965] p. 345). Even the most enthusiastic proponents of reform did not suggest that their plans could lead to the prevention of crime, let alone insanity.

[78]See Lipson, pp. 74-80.

[79]Lipson, p. 80. James T. Crown has concluded that in New York the phrase was almost never used with the implication of a general reduction of state expenditures (James T. Crown, "The Development of Democratic Government in the State of New York Through the Growth of the Power of the Executive Since 1920" [Ph. D. dissertation, New York University, 1956], pp. 179-181).

[80]Though, to be sure, many placed an inordinate emphasis on them. This emphasis proved unfortunate as it enabled later critics of reorganization to attack reorganization on the grounds that it did not measure up to its claims of increased efficiency and economy. (Among others see William H. Edwards, "A Factual Summary of State Administrative Reorganization," Southwestern Social Science Quarterly 19 [June 1938]: 53-67; Charles S. Hyneman, "Administrative Reorganization: An Adventure into Science and Theology," Journal of Politics 1 [February 1939]: 62-75; and J. M. Jacobson, "Evaluating State Administrative Structure—the Fallacy of the Statistical Approach," American Political Science Review 22 [November 1928]: 928-935.) The movement as a whole might have been better off had it emphasized what one reorganization advocate did:

"Those who sanguinely suppose that either of these reforms [budget reform or administrative reorganization] is going to result in any . . . very substantial reduction of expenditures are . . . doomed to disillusionment . . . the margin of possible saving even in the most scientific of budgets is relatively small. . . . To my mind its importance would lie not in the comparatively small saving of dollars or improvement of service, but in the example of orderliness, and decency and of sense of responsibility which the government ought to set." (Howard L. McBain, "The Problem of Governmental Reorganization," *Proceedings of the Academy of Political Science* 9 [New York, July 1921]: 332-333.)

[81] Albert Stickney, *Organized Democracy* (Boston: Houghton Mifflin and Co., 1906), p. 35.

[82] Howe, p. 7.

[83] John M. Mathews, *Principles of American State Administration* (New York: D. Appleton and Co., 1917), p. 502.

[84] In fact the addition of the reorganization writers to the ranks of the deprecators of separation of powers helped ensure that by the end of the first decade of the 20th century, "The traditional doctrine of separation of powers had become the bete noir of American political science . . ." (Waldo, p. 36).

[85] Quoted in Henry L. Stimson, "The Principle of Responsibility in Government," *Proceedings of the Academy of Political Science* 5 (New York, October 1914): 23-24.

[86] See Lipson, pp. 68-69. On these and on other "arguments by analogy" used by the reorganization writers, see also Crown, pp. 159-175.

[87] Woodrow Wilson, "The Study of Public Administration," *Political Science Quarterly* 2 (1887): reprint ed., 56 (December 1941): 493.

[88] Charles A. Beard, "Reconstructing State Government," *New Republic* 24 (August 21, 1915): p. 9.

[89] Richard S. Childs, "The Short Ballot," *Outlook* 92 (July 17, 1909): 635-639. It is Childs' belief that he was the first to use the term. (Interview with Mr. Richard S. Childs, Brooklyn, New York, August 21, 1974).

[90] Childs, p. 636.

[91] Beard, "The Ballot's Burden," *Political Science Quarterly* 24 (December 1909): 636.

[92] Ibid., pp. 600-601.

[93] Idem. "Reconstructing State Government," p. 9.

[94] Walker D. Hines, "Our Irresponsible State Governments," *Atlantic Monthly*, May 1915, pp. 637-638.

[95] Leonard D. White, *Introduction to the Study of Public Administration* (New York: The Macmillan Co., 1926), pp. 191-192.

[96] Jesse Burkhead, *Government Budgeting* (New York: John Wiley and Sons, Inc., 1956), p. 22.

[97] William F. Willoughby, *The Problem of a National Budget* (New York: D. Appleton and Co., 1918), p. 31.

[98] Beard, "Reconstructing State Government," p. 1.

[99] Croly, "State Political Reorganization," p. 134.

[100] Mathews, p. 502.

[101] Abernathy, p. 7.

[102] Bryant Putney, "Reorganization of State Governments," *Editorial Research Reports* 1 (May 1938): 304.

[103] Luther Gulick, "Effective State Government: A Problem of Organization," *State Government* 12 (June 1939): 110.

[104] As early as 1872 Governor John T. Hoffman complained that:

"Under the existing constitution, the executive department of the state is not so organized as to insure the most efficient administration of affairs, and the most complete and direct responsibility. . . . The governor ought to be held responsible for every branch of the actual administration of the state's affairs. Under our present constitution all the important departments are separated from his control" (Charles Z. Lincoln, ed., *Messages from the Governors*, 11 vols. [Albany; J. B. Lyon Co., 1909], 6:395-396).

Among the governors following Hoffman who complained of one or another aspect of the fragmented state administrative system were Governor David Hill (David Hill, *The Public Papers of David Hill* [Albany; The Argus Co., Printers, 1886], p. 38) and Governor Roswell P. Flower (Roswell P. Flower, *The Public Papers of Roswell P. Flower* [Albany: The Argus Co., Printers, 1892], p. 20).

[105]Charles Evans Hughes, *The Public Papers of Charles Evans Hughes* (Albany: J. B. Lyon Co., Printers, 1910), 3:8-9.

[106]Frank A. Updyke, "State Budgets," *American Political Science Review* 8 (February 1914): 59.

[107]An indication of the rapid growth of the number of "advocates" is the testimony of Arthur Ludington, Childs' assistant, concerning this growth in the National Organization. At the time of the organization's first annual banquet in January 1910, Ludington counted 300 such "advocates," while in February 1911, there were 11,000 (Arthur Ludington, "Progress of Short Ballot Movement." *American Political Science Review* 5 [February 1911]: 83).

Chapter 2

Preparation for the Convention

The New York State Constitutional Convention of 1915, by virtue of both the manner in which it was called and its composition, seemed, on its eve, unlikely to result in recommendations for radical changes of any kind. To the casual observer as well as to some of the participants, any suggestion that the convention would prove to contribute significantly to the reform of the state executive would have seemed unwarranted. Certainly, the suggestion that upon its conclusion it would have, in Frederick C. Mosher's words, "... provided the ideological fodder and stimulated the reformist fervor for most of the significant changes in New York State government in the next three decades",[1] would have been met with disbelief.

THE CALL FOR A CONVENTION

The 1915 convention was called for reasons wholly unconnected with the issue of executive reorganization. The last constitutional convention had been held in 1894 and, by provision of that convention,[2] the voters were not scheduled to pass on the desirability of holding another one until 1916. Instead, Governor Martin Glynn, on behalf of the Democrats, raised the issue in 1912. Glynn argued that the question of holding a constitutional convention should be put to the voters in 1914, which, unlike 1916, was a non-presidential election year, and would therefore serve to pre-

35

vent a confusion of state and national issues. Putting the question in 1915 would also not do for the voters would still be required to vote on the amendments the convention produced in the general election of 1916. This was the stated reasons the Democrats sought to move up the date of the constitutional convention question. In fact, there was another, less disinterested, motivation.

The 1894 convention had been controlled by the Republicans[3] and the product of its work, the prevailing state constitution, thoroughly reflected this control. In no area was this more true than in that of apportionment, where the constitution distinctly favored the Republicans.[4] Unable to prevent its passage in the convention, the Democrats bitterly denounced the apportionment provision on every occasion since 1894 and anxiously awaited an opportunity to rewrite it. The opportunity was long in coming, however, for Republican control of the state continued through the first decade of the twentieth century. Finally, in 1912, an opportunity arose. That year found the Republicans badly splintered by the inroads of the Progressives. Nationally, the party fell to third place on the ballot when it failed to carry any states except Utah and Vermont. Locally, the Democrats controlled both the statehouse and the legislature. The Democrats concluded that the chances for a Democratic controlled constitutional convention had never been better. This was the reason they called for an early vote on the question of holding a constitutional convention. Their concern over the dangers of popular confusion of national and local issues was but a convenient pretext; the real reason was far less high minded and nonpartisan.[5]

In December of 1913 the Democratic legislature voted to move up the date of the constitutional convention question to early 1914, and on April 7, 1914, the voters approved a convention. The margin by which it was approved, however, was very narrow. The issue of holding a constitutional convention had apparently not interested many people and the turnout on both sides of the question was small. The total number of votes cast, 305,291, stands in striking contrast to the number of votes cast in the 1912 gubernatorial election, 1,611,672.[6] With few exceptions, the strong Republican counties voted against a convention by votes of from two to five, to one; but Tammany Hall's efforts in New York City helped the proposition through. The convention carried by a slight 1,353 vote margin.[7]

The motivation behind the call for a constitutional convention at this time, the general lack of interest in a convention, and the narrow margin by which one was approved, certainly did not suggest that fundamental changes, except perhaps in the area of apportionment, would be undertaken by the convention. The next step towards the convention, the selection of delegates, seemed to ensure that no such changes would take place.

THE DELEGATES

Some major changes took place in the relative strength of the Republican and Democratic parties from the time the Democrats began agitating for a constitutional convention in 1912 until the selection of delegates to the convention at the general election of 1914. The position of the Democrats in 1914 was not nearly as strong as it was in 1912. The small margin by which the convention had been approved was only the most recent evidence of this. The difficulties of the party dated from an event which occurred in 1912 and whose potential for long-range harm had been seriously underestimated by the Democrats at the time. This was the impeachment of Governor William Sulzer.[8] While the official charges against Sulzer had concerned, among other things, his failure to report campaign contributions, his real sin was that he refused to cooperate with Tammany boss Charles Murphy in the time honored tradition of Democratic governors. Murphy's revenge was the only impeachment and conviction of a governor in New York's history.

Uncooperative to the end, Sulzer did not go quietly. He denounced Tammany and framed the issue of his impeachment as a struggle between the forces of law and those of corruption and dirty politics. This view of the impeachment evoked wisespread sympathy throughout the state. For while there was little doubt as to his guilt on the official charges, it was clear that Sulzer was being punished first and foremost for his lack of fealty to Murphy. The first major test of the extent to which the Sulzer affair had damaged the party came in the 1913 elections, and the results showed that the damage had been considerable. Statewide, the Democrats lost control of the Assembly—among those elected to the Assembly was Sulzer himself, running on the Progressive line. In local contests numbers of Democratic controlled cities were lost, including Albany and, in the greatest blow, New York City. The New York City mayoralty election saw Fusion candidate John Purroy Mitchell sweep into office carrying every borough. In addition, Fusion won control of the board of aldermen and the board of estimate. This was the popular response to the Sulzer impeachment.[9]

Hoping that the negative reaction to the impeachment had run its course in the 1913 elections, the Democrats proceeded with their plans for a constitutional convention. They still hoped to control the convention, counting on the schism in the Republican party provided by the Progressives.[10] However, when in early 1914 the convention was approved by only the narrowest of margins, it became apparent to them that the consequences of the Sulzer affair were far more serious than they had thought.[11] For the first time since they had broached the subject in 1912, the Democrats began to have serious doubts as to who would control the constitutional convention. These doubts grew as it became clear that the gubernatorial election of 1914, at which time delegates to the convention would also be chosen, would pit popular Republican New York District Attorney Charles Whitman against Governor Martin Glynn, the man who was widely perceived to have gained most from Sulzer's misfortune by having been elevated from the lieutenant governorship upon the latter's impeachment.

The election of delegates to the constitutional convention was thus viewed with a good deal of trepidation by the Democrats. One result of this trepidation was that they took the precaution of running their leaders as candidates for delegates from safe Tammany districts and not for delegates at large[12]—there were to be 153 district delegates and 15 delegates at large[13]—a designation usually given prominent politicians. Not so the Republicans. Buoyed by the results of the 1913 elections, the narrow approval granted the constitutional convention, and the prospect of running with the popular Whitman, they designated as candidates for delegates at large the best known men in the party. As it happened, the Democrats' precaution was a wise one. In a landslide victory that fall, which saw the Republicans gain control of the governor's office and the legislature, 116 Republican delegates to the constitutional convention were elected and only 52 Democrats. Among the winners were all 15 of the Republican candidates for delegates at large.

Among the delegates-elect were the leading men of both parties. For the Democrats they included: Morgan J. O'Brien, elder statesman of the party and a former state supreme court justice; William F. Sheehan, a former lieutenant governor; Delancey Nicoll and John B. Stanchfield, leading attorneys; and the three Tammany Hall stalwarts, Al Smith and Robert F. Wagner, both of whom were just beginning their illustrious careers but had already served terms as speaker of the Assembly and lieutenant governor, respectively, and James A. Foley, Charles Murphy's son-in-law and a man greatly respected in his own right who would later earn the characterization, ". . . most respected surrogate judge in the nation."[14] It was these men whom the party successfully protected by running as district delegates. The 15 Republican delegates at large read like a roster of the most prominent figures in the New York State Republican party. These included: Elihu Root, elder statesman and former secretary of war, secretary of state, and United States senator; Henry L. Stimson, former secretary of war; George W. Wickersham, former United States attorney general; Seth Low, former mayor of New York City and president of Columbia University; Herbert Parsons; a former congressman and leader of the New York County republicans; John Lord O'Brian, a former United States attorney; Louis Marshall, one of the leading constitutional lawyers of the day; and Jacob Gould Schurman, president of Cornell University. In addition, Frederick C. Tanner, Republican state chairman, and his immediate predecessor in that post, William Barnes, were both elected as district delegates.

The delegates included a large number of experienced and talented men. Of the 168, 39 had had previous legislative experience: one in the United States Senate; three in the United States House of Representatives; 14 in the New York State Senate; and 21 in the New York State Assembly. Three had filled United States Cabinet positions. Three had been United States attorneys. Two had been New York State lieutenant governors. Two had been candidates for governor in New York State. Thirteen had served as judges at one level or another.[15] Finally, four—Elihu Root, Louis Marshall, Delancey Nicoll, and Charles S. Mereness—had been delegates to the Constitutional Convention of 1894. Though they represented various professions, the overwhelming majority (calculated at different times and by different people at 118,[16] 125,[17] 126,[18] and 134[19]) were members of the legal profession. Among these were many of the leading corporate and constitutional lawyers of the state. Of the non-lawyers, there were college presidents, physicians, journalists and representatives of various other professions and the business world.[20] Together, they comprised an extremely able group. In a post-mortem offered soon after the convention, delegate Jacob Gould Schurman attested to the fact that "the average of ability and intelligence of the delegates was very high."[21] Years later, two other delegates reflected on the quality of the members of the convention. John Lord O'Brian recalled the "extraordinarily large number of truly eminent men"[22] in the convention, and Frederick C. Tanner stated that "the personnel of the Constitutional Convention of 1915 was, I think,

commonly regarded as one of the highest class—both from the point
of experience and ability—that had ever been held to pass on
constitutional questions."[23]

But if the delegates were characterized by experience and ability,
they also shared another characteristic, their conservatism. The
delegates consisted of Democrats and Republicans exclusively.
The Progressive party had run candidates for delegates but had
failed to elect a single one. Organized labor too had been all but
shut out of the convention. Two of its representatives, Samuel
Gompers and Labor Commissioner Lynch, had run as at large
delegates on the Democratic ticket; while two, Homer Call and
John Mitchell, had been at-large candidates on the Progressive
ticket, and several others ran as district delegates. In the end, only
three district delegates, Richard H. Curran, James H. Dahn, and
Patrick J. Tierney, were elected.

Both the Republican and Democratic parties had contributed to
the convention not only their ablest men, but also some of their
most conservative. The leaders of both parties in the convention, as
well as the great majority of the rank and file, were men of wealth
and position who were eager to preserve the status quo. Excepting
a very few, not a man among them had been identified with
progressive causes or movements aimed at changing the organization or functions of government. The assessment of Stanley Isaacs, a
Progressive party leader in 1915 and chairman of that party's
constitutional convention committee, that "the Constitutional Convention . . . was controlled by the most conservative people in the
Republican Party allied with the most conservative people in the
Democratic Party,"[24] was not the bitter, partisan reaction of one
whose party was unrepresented in the convention. It was, in fact, an
accurate appraisal of the membership, or at least the influential
membership, of the convention. William Barnes, a conservative
Republican delegate on the opposite side of the political spectrum
from Isaacs, wrote to Elihu Root before the convention met that he
had studied its membership and had arrived at a conclusion
regarding the Republican, or controlling members:

> I have studied the convention with a great deal of care, in order to get
> what seems to be its psychology. I find the most noteworthy feature
> of it is the intense conservatism of most of the Republican mem-
> bers.[25]

Whether one approved of it, as did Barnes, or disapproved, as did
Isaacs, it was clear that the nature of the membership of the
convention in general, and of its leadership in particular, was a
conservative one.

The makeup of the convention suggested several things about its probable course and character. To begin with, it would, of course, be a Republican convention. With a 64-vote edge, the Republicans would not only command large, automatic majorities on questions of interest to both parties, but would also control the convention presidency and committee chairmanships. Second, the work of the convention would, in all probability, be of high quality. The experience and ability of its members would ensure a high level of sophistication in its approach to problems and a high level of discourse in its deliberations. Last, and most important to the kind of document the convention would ultimately produce, the convention, it seemed certain, would be a conservative one. The conservatism of the membership, Republican and Democratic alike, suggested that it was highly unlikely that the convention would result in recommendations for major changes in any area. On the contrary, it seemed likely that the great majority of the convention would oppose recommendations for fundamental change.

The conclusion suggested by the conservative nature of the membership seemed to confirm what had been suggested earlier by the manner in which the convention had been called—no fundamental changes would be undertaken by the convention. And to the casual observer this conclusion was entirely justified. There was, however, a third, less obvious factor to consider. This was the nature of the preparation for the convention. Far less visible, but all-important in setting the focus and establishing the tone of the convention, it was this factor which ultimately determined the course of its work.

PREPARATION FOR THE CONVENTION

Preparation for the convention took place on two different levels. One level was the formal and official one, mandated by the legislature and carried out by an appointed agency acting on behalf of the convention as a whole. The other level consisted of the informal and unofficial preparations of the convention members, acting on their own initiative on issues of interest to them as individuals. The two kinds of preparation, though carried out simultaneously, were, of course, separate efforts. Nevertheless, their results, as will be seen, strongly complemented each other and, together, held important consequences for the work of the convention. First, to an examination of each form of preparation.

PREPARATION BY THE CONSTITUTIONAL
CONVENTION COMMISSION

While both the aforementioned kinds of preparation are today commonly associated with constitutional conventions, and while unofficial preparations by convention members are no doubt as old as conventions themselves, official state preparation for a constitutional convention was, in 1915, a relatively new phenomenon. In the long history of state constitution making from 1776 to the early years of the twentieth century (127 state constitutions were enacted from 1776 to 1909[26]) little effort was made by the states to gather information and prepare reference materials for the use of delegates to constitutional conventions.[27] Where such preparation was made, primarily in the latter part of this period, it was almost always limited to purchase and distribution to delegates of collections of various state constitutions. In New York State, which led the states in recognizing the need for gathering and organizing information in advance of a constitutional convention[28]—New York had provided delegates to its constitutional conventions with compilations of state constitutions since the 1846 convention—an attempt was made as early as 1867 to go beyond supplying convention delegates with a mere collection of constitutions. The legislature directed that delegates to that year's constitutional convention were to be provided with a manual of information on the organization and finances of the state government. Unfortunately, the manual could not be prepared in time for the convention. For the 1894 convention, the legislature authorized the secretary of state, attorney general, and comptroller to appoint a body to prepare and supply to the delegates appropriate reference materials. Though the materials were duly prepared, a good portion of them was, again, not ready for the opening of the convention, and an even larger portion consisted of materials of little use to the delegates,[29] including a large collection of American state and foreign constitutions. In 1914, anticipating the following year's constitutional convention and determined to improve upon its 1867 and 1894 efforts, the legislature created a constitutional convention commission with a distinguished membership and charged it with directing preparations for the convention. The commission, consisting of the president of the Senate, the speaker of the Assembly, and three citizens appointed by the governor, was to "collect, compile, and print information and data . . . it may deem useful for the delegates . . . in their deliberations."[30] Conscious of the major shortcoming of the 1867 and 1894 preparations, the legislature added that "such information and data in printed form shall be supplied to . . . delegates before the opening of the convention and as soon as practicable after the same is printed."[31] The commission, as we shall see, proved successful in accomplishing its task, and because of the comprehensiveness, intelligence, and thoroughness of its work, marked a watershed in the history of preparations for constitutional conventions. With the completion of the commission's work, New York became "the first state to lay a solid research foundation for a constitutional convention,"[32] and her example has since been emulated by other states.

> Thorough research as a basis for constitution-making by conventions dates from 1915 when New York pioneered in collecting, analyzing, and presenting in readable form essential materials for the use of delegates to the convention held in that year. Since then practically every group concerned with comprehensive revision or formulation of a new constitution has grounded its recommendations on careful research.[33]

It was the primary objective of the constitutional convention commission, as it was the major focus of the unsuccessful 1867 and 1894 preparations, to prepare and provide the delegates with a thorough description of the organization and functions of the state government. To accomplish this, the commission turned to an existing state agency upon whom it came to rely for help in carrying out much of its work, the Department of Efficiency and Economy. A major part of the mandate of the department was to "make a careful and thorough study of each office, institution, and department maintained by the state"[34] with a view to determining where and what kinds of improvements could be made. The commission reasoned that the department could remain faithful to its own mandate and at the same time provide valuable assistance to the commission. The department agreed, and, at the request of the commission, undertook a comprehensive study of the state government machinery.

It was the policy of the department to secure the services of experts on the projects it worked on. For its study of the state government machinery, the department requested the help of the New York Bureau of Municipal Research. Though the bureau was then a relatively new organization—it had been incorporated in 1907—it had, by 1914, undertaken studies pertaining to government organization in over 50 cities.[35] The bureau responded most generously, assigning to the department, free of charge, a group of 20 men headed by Charles A. Beard and Frederick A.

Cleveland. The staffs of the department and the bureau were merged, and though the study would be carried out, and its findings ultimately presented, by the department, it was clear that the bureau, by virtue of its experience and expertise, would be responsible for the overall direction of the study.

The study was carried out by eliciting descriptive information from each of the state's numerous departments, offices, boards, and commissions. This information included the agencies' functions, organization, activities, number of employees, and salary cost. To ensure uniformity in the manner in which the agencies would respond, each agency was issued special forms prepared by the bureau, accompanied by instructions on how to complete them, and sample sheets. Staff members were sent to each agency to aid them in collecting, compiling, and recording the requested data. Based on the information obtained in this manner, written and graphic descriptions were prepared on each department, office, board, and commission in the state. For the purposes of the final report, all the agencies were divided into 12 functional groupings. These were: legislative, executive, administrative, judicial, regulative, defensive, agricultural, educational, public works, conservation and custodianship, celebrative and commemorative, and care of delinquents, defectives, and dependents. The descriptions of each agency appeared under the heading of the grouping to which it was assigned.

The final report was a massive 768-page, comprehensive, and detailed description of the organization and functions of the state government. By its own description, and there is no evidence to dispute the claim, it was "the first complete description of a state government that has ever been prepared."[36] The department submitted the report to the commission on January 15, 1915, and the commission was satisfied that it had met its goal of preparing a thorough reference work on the state government for the use of the delegates.

THE SECOND STEP: AN APPRAISAL

In accepting the report of the Department of Efficiency and Economy, the constitutional convention commission received a straight, factual description of the state government. Excepting some brief introductory remarks, the report made no attempt to evaluate the system it described. This, of course, was just what the commission had sought, concerned foremost as it was with providing the delegates with a reference work. Now, with the reference work completed, and with several months left until the opening of the convention on the sixth of April, the commission decided to go beyond this to the preparation of a second report which would evaluate the organization and functions of the state government and make appropriate recommendations. As the Department of Efficiency and Economy was to be phased out in a matter of weeks—it was abolished by the legislature on March 2, 1915—it would not be available for this second study. The commission asked the Bureau of Municipal Research if it would undertake the work alone and the bureau agreed to do so.

It was not difficult to predict the general nature and thrust of the bureau's evaluation. One important clue was had in the aforementioned introduction to the descriptive report coauthored by the bureau. Brief as it was, the introduction made it abundantly clear that it was dissatisfied with the prevailing structure of the state government. Noting numerous outstanding inconsistencies and duplications throughout the state government machinery,[37] it observed that: "The entire structure of the State government, as it now exists, may be said to have grown from year to year rather than to have been builded according to any studied plan of scientific or economic needs."[38]

It was thus logical to assume that the bureau's evaluation would call for some kind of reorganiztion of the state government. An even better clue, however, to the kind of evaluation the bureau would produce, lay in the basic philosophy of the bureau. It was evident from some of the key principles of this philosophy that the bureau shared a common orientation to the problems of government with that of the state reorganization movement. The leaders of the bureau were, in Dwight Waldo's phrase, "apostles of 'the efficiency idea.' "[39] They stressed the need for efficiency and economy in government and cited as one of the major reasons for the bureau's establishment, the contribution it could make in promoting such efficiency and economy. In order to infuse efficiency and economy into government, the bureau urged the adoption of the business model. It looked upon the principles and skills employed in the private sector as neutral ones, equally applicable and potentially of great benefit to the public sector. One feature of the business model that would be particularly useful for government was the concept of centralized authority with responsibility invested in the single chief executive. These principles of the bureau's philosophy, briefly stated here,[40] were, of course, identical to the basic philosphy of the state reorganization movement. And, as we have seen, it was upon this philosophy that the reorganizers based their recommendations for change. It would therefore come as no surprise if the bureau, whose work had focused primarily on municipal government, would, in turning to the problems of New York State government, produce an assessment and recommendations which would parallel the thinking of the reorganization movement.

The bureau completed its evaluation, submitted it to the constitutional convention commission, and shortly thereafter published it in its own journal, *Municipal Research*,[41] under the title, "The Constitution and Government of the State of New York: An Appraisal." While it was presented as the work of the bureau as a whole, with no specific authorship cited, it was, in fact, the work of Frederick A. Cleveland and Charles A. Beard.[42] As expected, the "Appraisal" did call for a reorganization of the state government and its reasoning did parallel the thinking of the state reorganization movement. In fact, it was a complete statement of the movement's theory and aims.

The "Appraisal" began by stating its view of the principle upon which American state government was originally established:

> . . . American state government, in its essential principles, was not originally designed for efficient, constructive public work, but was the product of temporary and peculiar conditions growing out of the revolt against Great Britain. In their natural antipathy to leadership by a royal agent, the revolutionists rejected leadership altogether. In their fear of the British crown and the royal governor they came to fear all power, even if exercised by their own agents. Instead of making the executive authority responsible, therefore, they shackled it. Knowing that royal agents could not be entrusted with authority, they came to the conclusion that no one could be entrusted with authority. Their ideal of government was a negative one and in seeking after a government powerless to do harm they set up one weak in power for good.[43]

It was from the legacy of this history, asserted the "Appraisal," that the modern state suffered:

> This principle of negation, of preventing evil by dividing the powers of government into numerous parts is the chief source of the wastefulness, irresponsibility, and inefficiency which characterize the present system of government.[44]

The "Appraisal" cited numerous examples of this wastefulness, irresponsibility, and inefficiency in the New York State government, among them: the multiplicity of independent, elected executive officers; the 169 uncoordinated departments, offices, boards, and commissions, whose functions often overlapped; and the 16 different methods of appointment of executive officers and the seven different methods of removal.[45] It then suggested what would be required to eliminate this wastefulness, irresponsibility, and inefficiency:

> It is clear that the problem presented here involves more than a mere readjustment of parts—a rearrangement of powers and of departments, bureaus, and divisions of the administration. In fact it goes to the very root of the whole system of government. Responsiveness and responsibility for economy and efficiency cannot be secured by administrative alterations alone. They can only be obtained by a fundamental readjustment of the relations between the legislature and the governor on the one hand and between the governor and the administrative officers on the other.[46]

The fundamental readjustment of these relationships can only be brought about, argued the "Appraisal," by a proper understanding of the nature of representative government. It is a fundamental principle of democratic governments that the public business be managed as a trust. Representative government is the institutional form which expresses this principle, it being adopted in order to assure the governed that the government's power shall be exercised and its funds expended for the common good. In this sense, representative government is comparable to a joint stock company; they are both incorporated trusteeships in which many are interested. This being the case, it is entirely appropriate for representative governments to look to the management of the ordinary joint stock company to see if any of its features are applicable to its own situation.

The two key requirements of any trust, asserted the "Appraisal," whether it be a joint stock company or a representative government, are responsiveness and responsibility; responsiveness to the will of its membership and responsibility to the members for its activities. In the case of the joint stock company, responsiveness and responsibility are ensured by the presence of two features characteristic of such companies. They are: (1) the selection of a person or body as the executive, charged with carrying on the day to day business of the company, and (2) the selection of trustees, charged with reviewing the activities of the executive and expressing their approval or disapproval. The authority of the executive in directing the business of the company and in taking steps to ensure its efficient operation is unquestioned. Equally unquestioned is the authority of the trustees to hold the executive answerable for his activities. Responsiveness to the will of the company's members is thus ensured by granting the executive the authority to carry out this will, and responsibility for the company's activities is ensured by making the executive answerable for these activities. In the same way that these two features provide responsiveness and responsibility in the joint stock company, argued the "Appraisal," their presence in a representative government would ensure its responsiveness and responsibility. In fact, it submitted, in those governments where these features are present—notably Great Britain, whose system of cabinet government fits the metaphor of the joint stock company best—responsiveness and responsibility are also present. Conversely, where these features are not present in a representative government, neither responsiveness nor responsibility will be present, and this is the case in New York State government and in American state government generally.

The state chief executive, owing to the American "doctrine of 'original sin' in politics, that no one can be safely entrusted with any substantial authority,"[47] has never been granted the authority to conduct the business of the state. His powers have been diluted and divided to the point where he lacks the means to carry out the will of the people. For this reason he cannot be responsive to their needs. Nor, by the same token, can he be held responsible for the activities undertaken by the executive in conducting the business of the state. For there are others who share executive powers over whom he has no control and for whose activities he is therefore not answerable. Thus has the state, by refusing to provide for a real chief executive—for despite his constitutional title, "one hundred and thirty-eight years of political experience has demonstrated the inadequacy of mere declarations to make a chief executive"[48]— provided for unresponsiveness and irresponsibility.

If responsiveness and responsibility are to be had in the state government, argued the "Appraisal," the example of business must be followed. The state must create a chief executive in whom authority and responsibility are concentrated. To accomplish this, the state's administrative system must be reorganized in such a way as to place the chief executive at its center and to make him its guiding force. Only through adoption of such a reorganization would the state chief executive be given the means to be responsive to the needs of the people and only then could he be held responsible for meeting those needs.

The arguments and conclusions of the "Appraisal" were, of course, similar to those made by other reorganization writings.[49] This is true even of its specific recommendations. For while the "Appraisal" did not offer a detailed plan for reorganization, choosing to wait until the convention had assembled when it could present such a plan to the appropriate committees,[50] it did indicate what the essential features of the reorganization should be. These included a consolidation of administrative agencies, a short ballot, and an executive budget. Nevertheless, the "Appraisal" was different in one important respect. Unlike other writings of the reorganization movement, the "Appraisal" came after, and was based upon, an exhaustive study of a state government, the earlier study carried out by the bureau and the Department of Efficiency and Economy. It was thus not only a statement of the reorganization movement's theory and aims, but one which could legitimately claim a solid basis in research. For this reason, it could be expected to be a more effective argument for reorganization. Just how effective it was would be determined, of course, by the reaction of the report's recipients.

The bureau submitted the "Appraisal" to the constitutional convention commission and received the commission's thanks. It did not, however, receive an endorsement of its work. The commission saw itself as a neutral service agency of the convention, authorized merely to "collect, compile, and print information" for the use of the delegates, and not to become an active advocate of one position or another. Thus, the commission did not consider it appropriate to evaluate the recommendations of the "Appraisal." Instead, it sent copies of the work, as it had done with the earlier descriptive report, to the delegates, explaining that it bore no responsibility for the opinions expressed therein.

Having sent the delegates copies of the descriptive report and the "Appraisal," the commission completed the bulk of its work. The commission had initiated preparation of other materials[51] in addition to the works of the Department of Efficiency and Economy and the Bureau of Municipal Research, but these two works were by far the most significant and together they formed the core of the commission's preparation. It now remained for the delegates to study the materials, form their own conclusions, and decide on a course of action in the convention. Not that they had been relying solely on the preparations undertaken by the commission. For the delegates themselves had engaged in preparatory work.

PREPARATION BY THE DELEGATES

Preparation for the convention by the delegates was limited largely to the Republicans. The Democratic delegates, greatly outnumbered as they were, recognized the futility of formulating a program for the convention. Such a program would only be dismissed by the Republican dominated convention. Far more appropriate for them was to adopt a posture of watchful waiting with a view to protecting, so far as they could, their own interests from the plans of the majority opposition. The plans of the majority were not, however, easily arrived at. For the Republicans, the convention presented an opportunity to assess the relative strengths and shortcomings of the 1894 constitution and to either reaffirm their faith in the document or recommend changes, large or small. But different delegates could be expected to have different perceptions of the state's problems and of how well the prevailing constitution enabled it to cope with those problems. Arriving at some consensus and achieving a degree of unity constituted a large part of the preconvention work of the Republications.

HENRY L. STIMSON'S ROLE

One delegate who had very definite ideas concerning the direction that the convention should take was Henry L. Stimson. After long and serious reflection over a period of several years on the problems of the state government, Stimson had arrived at certain conclusions. He now saw the convention as the appropriate forum for articulating these conclusions and, ultimately, acting upon them. If the convention was to become such a forum, however, much preparatory work among the delegates was necessary. Stimson began this work far in advance of the convention. Through a combination of his own work and ability, the help of other delegates, and some fortuitous circumstances, he became the central figure in the Republican delegates' preparations for the convention.

Stimson had been the Republican candidate for governor in 1910 and, though he lost the election, he did not consider the effort a total waste. In a post-campaign letter to Charles Evans Hughes,[52] Stimson wrote that prior to running for governor his experience had been limited to the federal government—he had served as United States attorney for the southern district of New York from 1906-1909—and that as a consequence he had paid slight attention to state government issues. The campaign, he wrote, had educated him on the state government. His interest whetted by this experience, Stimson began reading widely on the subject of state government and corresponding with authorities in the field. Among the authorities he consulted were prominent state reorganization advocates such as Princeton Professor Henry J. Ford, who had contributed ideas to Stimson's gubernatorial campaign,[53] and Herbert Croly. Stimson was attracted to the arguments of the reorganization movement and was especially impressed with two basic principles of its philosophy. He recounted these in his autobiography, in a discussion of the development of his thinking in this late 1910, early 1911 period.[54] First, was the fact that the state governments were irresponsible:

> The difficulty faced by the public was that it was seldom easy to find out what official was responsible for any given success or failure. American Government in the early twentieth century was characterized by divided authority and general impotence; finding the sinner in politics was like finding the little round ball in the old shell game. The finger of blame was pointed by one office holder at another, right around the circle. . . . Nowhere could the voter stop his search and surely know who was his man. . . .[55]

The second principle was that if responsibility was to be had, as it surely must, authority must be concentrated:

> Responsibility could not be divorced from authority . . . irresponsibility was a direct result of scattered authority and divided power; fear of too much government had led to untrustworthy government. . . . The elected officials must have more power, not less—only so could they be held accountable for success or failure.[56]

Stimson accepted these arguments and agreed that a reorganization based on these general premises was essential. He then turned to the particulars of such a reorganization and proceeded to formulate a specific plan for the reorganization of state governments.

Stimson unveiled his plan in an address at the McKinley Day banquet of the Cleveland, Ohio, Tippecanoe Club on January 28, 1911. He had been urged to speak on the progressive movement within the Republican party and chose to focus on the attitude progressive Republicans should have towards the problems of state government. The theme of Stimson's address was that the states were in need of strong chief executives and, using the arguments of the reorganization advocates, he made a powerful case for the reorganization of state governments to this end. He specifically recommended adoption of a three point program which would enhance the power of the governor:

> (1) A lengthened term for the Governor; say four years. . . . (2) Give him the same power to select and control his cabinet and the heads of his departments which is possessed by the President of the United States, especially with an absolute and unconditional power of removal. This same power should be carried through all of the executive departments through which is administered the regulative control of our public service corporations and other public utilities,

52   THE NEW YORK STATE CONSTITUTIONAL CONVENTION

and (3) Give him the undisputed right, not only to suggest, but to frame and introduce his own legislative measures, giving to such measures a right of precedence on the legislative calendar.[57]

The first and third points of Stimson's program were not usually stressed—in some cases, not even mentioned—by most other reorganization advocates, especially the third which was radical even by reorganization standards. They emphasized three different items of which Stimson's speech hadn't made specific mention: consolidation of administrative agencies, a short ballot, and an executive budget.[58]

But the differences between Stimson's program and that of the other reorganization advocates were less substantive than differences in emphasis. The underlying principle of creating a powerful governor in whom authority was concentrated was identical to both programs. Moreover, within a short time after he offered his plan, certainly, as will be seen, by the time of the convention, Stimson came to include as highlights of his own plan administrative consolidation and an executive budget. The Cleveland address had been, by his own description "the first time [he had been] forced to organize his own mind"[59] on the subject. It generated an enormous amount of correspondence between Stimson and prominent politicians and scholars, all of which served to reinforce his thoughts concerning the necessity of reorganization and to convince him that the reorganization should include, in addition to the particulars he had emphasized, those emphasized by the other reorganization advocates.

Strongly as he felt the need for state reorganization, Stimson was realistic enough to recognize that his views were by no means commonly held[60] and that much work was to be done if reorganization was to be realized. "Nothing but the hardest and most constant of educational work can have any hope of preparing public sentiment for such a change by the time of our next Constitutional Convention,"[61] he wrote shortly after his Cleveland address. Yet, given the proper preparatory work, he did believe reorganization was attainable "by the time of our next Constitutional Convention." The convention he referred to was, of course, the one scheduled for 1916 and it was toward that date that Stimson planned. When the date of the convention was moved up to 1915, thus reducing the amount of time for Stimson's preparatory work by one year, his task became more formidable. Stimson was undaunted, however, in the face of this apparent setback and proceeded to adjust his plans and work toward an earlier convention. He could do so because he had, by then, made substantial progress in one important area of his preparatory work. This area consisted of winning the support of the New York Republican party's universally respected elder statesman, Elihu Root, for reorganization.

STIMSON AND ROOT

Stimson enjoyed no small stature in his party. His was an influential and respected voice, whether the subject was state reorganization or any other issue. His stature could not compare, though, with that of Elihu Root. Like Stimson, Root had been, by the early years of the second decade of the century, a former United States attorney for the southern district of New York (1883-1885) and secretary of war (1899-1901). In addition, he had been secretary of state (1901-1909) and was United States senator from New York (1909-1915). He had been at the center of national Republican politics for many years and even enjoyed an international reputation, winning the Nobel Peace Prize in 1913. Distinguished New York Republican contemporaries spoke of Root in superlative tones often approaching awe. John Lord O'Brian called him "brilliant beyond description at times" and declared that "Mr. Root was the greatest man I have ever known in my lifetime."[62] Jacob Gould Schurman believed "he is undoubtedly the ablest man we have in public life today."[63] And James W. Wadsworth, Root's successor in the United States Senate, asserted that Root possessed the "best legal mind in the country"[64] and that "he was a philosopher and a prophet."[65] These comments were entirely representative of the esteem in which most New York Republicans held Root.

The esteem in which Root was held was sufficient reason to assume that he would play a leading role in the Republican involvement in any state constitutional convention. There was, however, an even better reason. This was his role in the 1894 convention. Root had been chairman of the judiciary committee and served in that post with distinction. One scholar of that conventon described Root's work in the following manner:

> At the head of the Judiciary Committee was E. Root, whose infinite capacity for labor added to his great abilities and acquirements as a lawyer enabled him to impress himself upon the work of the convention to an extent unapproached by any other member of that body.[66]

Even more important than his committee chairmanship was the position he held as floor leader. As floor leader, Root was second only to convention President Joseph Choate in the overall running of the convention. Having distinguished himself in his assigned area of work and having had the experience of holding the second most important position in a constitutional convention, there was little question that the Republicans would grant Root a pre-eminent position of leadership in the next convention.

Stimson appreciated Root's status in the Republican party. Indeed, Stimson himself had the highest regard for Root, referring to him as the "greatest American" he had ever known.[67] Stimson understood that if reorganization was to make any headway at the next constitutional convention, whenever it came, it was important that he win Root's sympathy for it. In attempting to win Root's support for reorganization, Stimson had two factors in his favor. One was his personal relationship with Root and the other was the particular political climate of the years 1900-1915.

Stimson and Root were extremely close personally and professionally. Their relationship dated back to 1891 when, upon passing the bar examination, Stimson was offered a clerkship in the prestigious law firm of (Elihu) Root and Clarke. One year after accepting the clerkship, Stimson was offered, and accepted, a junior partnership in the firm. Stimson and Root were immediately attracted to each other and the older man took the younger under his wing, teaching him law and instructing him in the ways of politics. Root became an enormous influence on Stimson's life; an influence, Stimson maintained, second only to that of Stimson's father:

> To no man, save his own father, Stimson frequently acknowledged, did he owe as much intellectually and morally; and the father himself once admitted that, were it not for his own admiration for Root, he would be jealous of the hold he had over his son.[68]

As he did professionally, so did Stimson follow in Root's footsteps in public service, serving in two of the same positions previously held by the latter: United States attorney for the southern district of New York—his appointment to which post Root had more than a little to do with[69]—and secretary of war.[70]

Needless to say, the relationship was not all one-sided, with Root as mentor and Stimson the eager student. Through the years, Root came to rely on Stimson professionally and politically and he respected the latter's views, especially in areas which which he himself was relatively unfamiliar. That Stimson had studied the issue of state government reorganization thoroughly and had concluded that it was a necessity was bound to impress Root. This would have been true even if there were no other reasons for Root to be favorably disposed to reorganization. In fact, there was such a reason. Ever since the Republican debacle of 1912, Root had been convinced of what his biographer referred to as ". . . the necessity of having the Republican party stand for principles which would meet the popular unrest to which the Progressives appealed without going the length of what they considered the unsound proposals which Roosevelt had sponsored."[71] Root understood that the welfare of the Republican party depended on its ability to retain progressive Republicans. To this end, the party would simply have to adjust its policies without changing its essential character. The question was which policies to adopt. With Root grasping at progressive straws, it was an especially auspicious time for him to be introduced to the issue of state reorganization.

It is difficult to determine at precisely what point in time Stimson won Root over to the reorganization,[72] but it is certain that it was sometime between the Republican defeat of November 1912 and December 5, 1913. The latter date was the one for which a meeting of leading New York Republicans was called by Root, State Chairman Barnes, and 11 Republican members of New York's congressional delegation and of the Republican national committee for the purpose of defining the principles for which the party stood in the post-1912 election period. At the meeting, held at the Waldorf Astoria, Root came out vigorously for a number of measures, among them the short ballot and an executive budget. Whether it was because of Root's prestige in the party—and, to a lesser extent, Stimson's—or, as Root's biographer believes,[73] because no one else had an alternative program, or because the group believed in the measures, or a combination of the three, the measures were approved by the meeting.

Having won Root's support for reorganization and having gained the assent of the December meeting for some aspects of reorganization, Stimson could be justified in feeling that much positive movement had been made toward reorganization. Nevertheless, Stimson recognized that the approval of the December meeting was only a commitment in principle. Whether the leaders present at the meeting would support the short ballot and executive budget or other aspects of reorganization when it came to actually helping vote these measures into law remained to be seen. It also remained to be seen to what extent these leaders could influence others, and rank and file Republicans, toward reorganization. As it happened, the answers to these questions would soon be forthcoming. For just four months after the December meeting, on April 7, 1914, the voters approved a constitutional convention for 1915.

STIMSON'S PRE-CONVENTION PREPARATIONS

Once the result of the convention question vote became known, Stimson wasted no time. He began contacting key Republicans throughout the state, sounding them out on what subjects they felt the convention should deal with. He did not, in his communications with them press immediately for reorganization. He was far too sophisticated not to realize that his colleagues might resent being pressured so early on. Instead, he merely suggested areas which were of potential interest to the convention, among which, of course, was the issue of reorganizaton, and invited others to do the same.

On the eighth of May, Stimson sent letters to 25 of the most prominent Republicans in the state. The letters identified 12 subjects which Stimson felt the convention should take up, among them reorganization. To each of the 25 he suggested several of the 12 topics that they might investigate and then report on at a meeting of the Republican state committee scheduled for later that month. Most of the replies to his letters were encouraging, agreeing as they did that the 12 areas Stimson had identified would indeed be appropriate to the convention's work. An important exception, which was a portent of the opposition Stimson would later encounter from the upstate Republican establishment, was the reply of upstate Senator Elon Brown. Without commenting on any of the suggested topics, Brown replied that he wanted to caution against the convention's recommending major changes in any area. The convention had been approved by the narrowest of margins, he wrote, and thus possessed no real mandate for change.[74]

On the twenty-eighth of May, the Republican state committee met at the Waldorf Astoria under the chairmanship of Elihu Root. After a general discussion of what items the constitutional convention could deal with, Stimson moved that a committee of 25 persons be designated by Root for the purpose of constructing a list of issues to be taken up by the convention and formulating the Republican positions on those issues. The motion carried, as did another authorizing a state convention to be held in Saratoga on the eighteenth of August for the purpose of considering the document that the Committee of Twenty-five would produce. Within days after the meeting, Root asked Stimson for names of persons he would recommend for appointment to the committee.[75] While there is no record of the specific names Stimson recommended,[76] it is known that he urged Root not to appoint conservatives who would shy away from recommending fundamental changes in any area.[77]

That the group ultimately chosen by Root had a preponderance of progressive Republicans, such as Seth Low, Jacob Gould Schurman, John Lord O'Brian, Herbert Parsons, and Alphonse T. Clearwater, was in large part due, it can be safely assumed, to the input allowed Stimson by Root. In addition to selecting the members of the committee, Root chose a group of three from among the 25 to guide and direct the work of the larger group. The three were: Stimson, Seth Low, and William Guthrie, a distinguished Republican lawyer with a national reputation in the legal profession. This group called a meeting of the Committee of Twenty-five for the twenty-fourth of July.

Stimson was not content to rest until the first meeting of the Committee of Twenty-five. The focus of his activity in this period was an article he wrote on reorganization for *The Independent,*[78] a New York City weekly. The article was a summary of reorganization arguments and called on the constitutional convention to adopt the short ballot, executive budget and consolidation of executive agencies. It mentioned the fact that Elihu Root supported these measures. As with his first statement on behalf of reorganization three years earlier, Stimson's first public statement for reorganization since the constitutional convention had been called generated substantial reaction. Some of it, like that of upstate Republican Senator Edgar T. Brackett, was negative. Referring to the concentration of power in the governor that reorganization called for, Brackett wrote that "unrestrained power will make a wild beast of the most benevolent of men."[79] And then, in a later letter, he added:

> There is no government in the world so efficient as a pure, unlimited autocracy. It can hang a criminal quicker, build a dam quicker, put in any public improvement quicker, but, by God, it is at the expense of liberty, and liberty with a limited efficiency is infinitely preferred to autocratic ways coupled with no matter how great efficiency.[80]

Other reactions, like those of Alphonse T. Clearwater,[81] Jacob Gould Shurman,[82] and Seth Low, were positive; Low writing that he was "in hearty sympathy with every line of [the article]."[83] Much to Stimson's delight, the majority of responses was positive. The reactions, favorable and unfavorable, required replies, and much of Stimson's time in this period, before the meeting of the Committee of Twenty-five, was taken up in correspondence concerning the merits of his article.

One item of particular interest in his correspondence during this period was a letter he wrote to Frederick C. Tanner on the sixth of June. In this letter Stimson revealed his attitude toward the role of the Democrats in the coming convention. After argung the need for a greater concentration of executive authority, Stimson added: "I believe, too, that it is a solution peculiarly appropriate for the Republican Party to put forward, inasmuch as most of these evils are directly traceable to the counter Democratic policy of diffusion of responsibility."[84] In a later letter he sounded much the same theme:

> The issues which have interested me in the Constitutional Convention have been primarily those which divide the advocates of responsible from the advocates of irresponsible government and I have rather regarded the dividing line as a watershed between the Republican and Democratic Parties.[85]

This attitude was a curious one. Certainly the evidence did not suport it. In terms of "responsible government," there had been little difference between Republican and Democratic state administrations. Republicans, as a group, had not supported reorganization any more than had Democrats. The Democrats had their small share of reorganization advocates as did the Republicans.

Why did Stimson claim this was an issue of Republicans versus Democrats? One reason might be that he sincerely believed this was the case. A devoted Republican, then and for many years after, Stimson may have automatically associated what he believed to be the "right" side of any issue with the Republicans, and the "wrong" side with the Democrats. A better explanation may be that Stimson sought to make this an issue of party in order to enable him to urge fellow Republicans to close ranks and rally around a Republican cause. In this way he could appeal to those Republicans who were unsure of the merits of reorganization, per se, but had a stong sense of party loyalty. Whatever the explanation for his attitude, one thing is fairly certain—he lost little by adopting such a stance. His substantial prestige and influence was limited largely to Republican circles and any overtures he might have made to Democrats would not have been met with much enthusiasm. Moreover, Stimson was firmly convinced that it would be the Republicans who would dominate the convention.[86] While ignoring the Democrats might result in the loss of some support, it would be the large bloc of Republicans who would decide on the issues in the convention, and it was among this controlling group that Stimson chose to make his case.

On the twenty-fourth of July, the Committee of Twenty-five[87] met at Republican State Committee headquarters in New York City. Following a long, general, and inconclusive discussion of issues the convention might address, Stimson moved that a subcommittee of nine be appointed to draw up a draft proposal of issues and Republican positions which would then be reviewed by the whole committee several days before the state convention met on the eighteenth of August. This was promptly approved and Stimson was made the subcommittee's chairman. The committee agreed to meet at the United States Hotel in Saratoga on the evening of the fifteenth of August, and then adjourned.

The majority of the eight other members of the subcommittee[88] were progressive Republicans, the type of men Stimson had urged Root to appoint; indeed, it could well be that they owed their positions on the committee to Stimson's recommendations to Root.[89] Stimson would thus not have a particularly difficult time producing the kind of document he wanted. In fact, the only member of the sub-committee from whom Stimson encountered any serious opposition was William Guthrie. Not that this was unexpected. Stimson had long known Guthrie to be a staunch and unyielding conservative and had asked Root not to appoint Guthrie to the Committee of Twenty-five, arguing that "Guthrie is a dear friend of mine . . . but he is most distinctly reactionary on the problems of the state constitution."[90] Apparently Root felt he could not deny the widely respected lawyer and prominent Republican a place on the committee. Now, perhaps for similar reasons, Guthrie had been selected for the subcommittee. Guthrie's behavior bore out Stimson's worst fears. One fellow member of the subcommittee, John Lord O'Brian, later recalled Guthrie's behavior on the larger committee:

> Guthrie was one of the leaders of the New York bar and one of the great lawyers in the nation. . . . But he was really obnoxious in the deliberations of the Committee's work. He was argumentative and stubborn when he disagreed about something and exercised delaying tactics when he was opposed to something.[91]

Needless to say, his behavior was no better in the subcommittee and Stimson complained bitterly to Root of Grutrie's obstruction.[92] Apart from the difficulty with Guthrie, however, Stimson had a relatively free hand in directing the subcommittee's work.

Stimson assigned different issues to each member of the sub-committee to investigate and research. Based on this research, he and Seth Low wrote, circulated, and rewrote drafts of a comprehensive statement. By the third of August a final draft was had and on the sixth of August the document was sent to the members of the committee. The document[93] consisted of four main sections, one of which was entitled "Responsible Government." This section argued the need for a general concentration of authority in the governor and, to that end, recommended adoption of the short ballot, a consolidation of executive agencies, and a comprehensive state budget.[94] These recommendations represented by far the most revolutionary concepts in the entire document and it was, of course, this section which was most important to Stimson. It might, therefore, have been with some concern that Stimson passed the document on to the full committee for its consideration. But Stimson had reason to be optimistic. As in the subcommittee, the balance in the committee was weighted in favor of the progressives, again, a circumstance with which Stimson had more than a little to do, and this majority would ensure the committee's general receptivity to recommendations for change.

The deliberations of the full committee on the eve of the state convention went to Stimson's satisfaction. Guthrie and Brackett, the latter having been appointed to the committee by Root, it may be assumed, because of his considerable stature among upstate Republicans, were predictably opposed to the thrust of the entire section on "Responsible Government." The majority, however, was favorably disposed and, with a few minor changes, approved the document. The primary recommendations of the section on "Responsible Government," as revised and approved by the committee, read as follows:

> We recommend a substantial reduction in the number of elective officials by the application of the principle of the short ballot to the executive offices of the State.
>
> To prevent the multiplication of offices, we recommend that the various administrative functions of the State, so far as practicable, be vested in a limited number of departments. The present duplication of effort and expense in the public institutions of the State should be remedied by the establishment of a simpler and better organized system.
>
> We advocate the creation of more effective restraints upon the expenditure of public funds, and to the end (sic) the establishment of a system of official budgets.[95]

These were the recommendations the committee agreed to urge the state convention to adopt.

Revolutionary as they were, the chances of the convention approving these recommendations were excellent. While the 610 delegates to the convention represented a cross section of the party, including the most reactionary members, they could not fail to be impressed by the recommendations of the Committee of Twenty-five. The committee was, after all, composed of some of the most influential, if also most progressive, Republicans in the state and had spent much time studying and debating the issues. Their names as well as the expertise they had gained from their study of the issues would command the respect of the convention. Moreover, they had been handpicked by the revered Root and the product of their work had Root's blessing. This last factor was especially important as Root was to be chairman of the convention.

Up to this point, Root had not been much involved in any pre-constitutional convention activities, such as the work of the Committee of Twenty-five. As United States senator from New York, he had been preoccupied with national and, because of the war in Europe, international affairs. Responding in early August to one of Stimson's letters concerning constitutional convention matters, Root acknowledged that "it is hard just now to keep interested in anything except the war in Europe."[96] Now, as chairman of the state convention, Root would concentrate on issues pertaining to the party's pre-constitutional convention program, including the issue of state reorganization. Having come out for reorganization long ago, it could be expected that he would use his personal influence and leverage as chairman to get the convention to adopt the committee's recommendations.

One last factor would tend to increase the chances for approval by the convention. This was the fact that the document advanced by the committee was not, even if approved by the convention, binding on the delegates to the constitutional convention. The very first section of the document, inserted at the time of the subcommittee's initial draft, expressly stated that while the document would become the party's official pre-convention platform if approved by the state convention, it would not obligate Republican delegates to the constitutional convention to vote for all or any of its provisions. This feature of the document would certainly tend to make it less difficult for the state convention to approve it.

Along with the committee's document, the state convention received a minority report written by Brackett. Essentially, the report was an attack on the short ballot. It argued that granting the governor broad appointing powers was inconsistent with popular government and that such a move would be a step toward autocracy. Brackett was not without support in the convention. Indeed, he was joined there by three very formidable allies. These were: Elon Brown; William Barnes, the Republican state chairman; and Merton Lewis, the state's first deputy attorney general. Nevertheless, given the aforementioned factors operating in favor of the committee, he could not have been very hopeful that the convention would adopt his minority report.

It was perhaps for this reason that he did not concentrate on attacking the committee's recommendations in the convention as he did in the report. Instead, Brackett argued that the convention should allow the delegates to the constitutional convention an open mind. This could only be done, he said, by not approving any specific recommendations, thus not constraining the delegates to vote one way or another on any issue. His argument did not overlook the fact that the recommendations were not binding. Brackett acknowledged this, but asserted that for a practical matter it would make little difference whether they were binding or not:

> It is proposed in this platform formulated here in a body selected from all over the State without special reference to qualifications for considering the subject, to settle very basic questions of the State Government and to order the Constitutional Convention when convened to decide questions as here determined. I do not believe, Mr. Chairman and Gentlemen of this Convention, that this Convention is the proper place, nor that this is the proper time for the settlement of any such questions whatever. I am not aware (sic) that the language of one of the sections, which my friends in the rear will presently quote, disclaims any intention to instruct the delegates to the Constitutional Convention; but I am not unaware either, Mr. Chairman, of the fact that it is just by such insidious approaches that the members of the Constitutional Convention will feel themselves bound by any action that may be taken by this grand council of the party. It will be urged, as these questions are presented to the Constitutional Convention, that the party has spoken, and party pride and party loyalty will be appealed to that the provision here adopted by this Convention must be carried out.[97]

Brackett had, of course, an excellent point—indeed, this was precisely the objective of the authors of this "insidious approach." But the accuracy of his observation was either lost on, or ignored by, the convention. The convention rejected his arguments and approved the document as its pre-constitutional convention platform.

The acceptance by the state convention of the committee's document with its recommendations for reorganization marked the end of Stimson's active pre-constitutional convention work on behalf of reorganization. From the end of the summer until November, he was involved primarily in his campaign for election as a delegate at large to the convention. Then, after winning election, running third highest of the 15 successful candidates for delegates at large, Stimson made a conscious decision to curb his activities for reorganization. He communicated his reason for doing so in a December letter to Richard S. Childs:

> . . . since my election as constitutional delegate I have strongly felt that I must be very careful not to gain the position in the public mind of going into the convention as an avowed advocate of specific remedies. Such an advocate easily becomes recognized as a crank on his subject and if he reaches that unhappy position at once loses all his influence. Furthermore I think the people and the delegates rather expect their delegates to keep their minds open as to specific propositions of detailed remedies.[98]

Stimson's reasoning, which he reiterated in letters to others,[99] requires some explanation. Certainly, all who knew him knew he was a staunch reorganization advocate who felt reorganization was a priority item for the convention. Whether he liked it or not, he had already gained a "position in the public mind of going into the convention as an avowed advocate of specific remedies," and could not now claim to have an "open mind" concerning the need for specific reorganization measures. That Stimson himself was unaware of this is highly unlikely. A more plausible explanation is that what Stimson actually meant was that having gotten the party to go on record as favoring reorganization and having won over numbers of influential party people, including convention delegates, it was a good tactic to ease the pressure for the time being. Continuing the pressure for reorganization at this point could give Stimson the image of a singleminded fanatic or "crank," an image which would hardly command influence in the convention. The same concern for reorganization which had dictated a policy of outspokenness up to this point now dictated adoption of a low profile. And it was this policy of a low profile which Stimson maintained up to the convention.[100]

EFFECT OF THE PRE-CONVENTION PREPARATIONS

The pre-convention preparations of both the constitutional convention commission and the Republicans led by Stimson did not attract wide popular attention. While the products of their preparations—the works authored by the Department of Efficiency and Economy and the New York Bureau of Municipal Research, and the planks in the Republican party platform—were available to persons interested in the planning for the constitutional convention, the number of such persons was relatively small. The initial question of holding a convention did not, as we have seen, elicit much popular interest, and there was nothing to suggest that the situation had changed appreciably since that time. In fact, several convention delegates commented on the continued lack of public awareness of and interest in the convention. Charles H. Young mentioned this in a letter to Herbert Parsons shortly before their election as delegates-at-large:

> There is not one person in ten, in my experience, that knows there is a Constitutional Convention to be held. My second next door neighbor in New Rochelle did not know there was to be a convention, and did not know that I was a candidate, and this is not a particularly unintelligent or uninformed man.[101]

It was for this reason, and because of the earlier discussed factors of the manner in which the convention was called and the nature of its membership, both of which suggested that the convention would not result in recommendations for major changes of any kind,[102] that it could well have come as a surprise to large numbers of citizens when reorganization emerged as a major focus of the convention's work. For those people who were acquainted with the pre-convention preparations, however, such a development was not at all unexpected.

The pre-convention preparations ensured that reorganization would be an important issue in the convention. The reorganization recommendations of the Bureau of Municipal Research, though not specifically endorsed by the commission, formed a large and important part of the commission's official pre-convention materials which were supplied to all the delegates. The reorganization planks in the Republican party platform, though not binding on Republican convention delegates, nevertheless represented the official posture of the party regarding reorganization. Thus, if reorganization was not guaranteed by the pre-convention preparations, the issue of reorganization was at least assured of receiving serious attention. The common effect of both preparations was to ensure that reorganization would be considered and debated by the convention. The final result of this consideration and debate would depend, of course, on the work of the proponents of reorganization in the convention.

NOTES

[1]Frederick C. Mosher, "The Executive Budget, Empire State Style," *Public Administration Review* 12 (Spring 1952):78.

[2]The 1894 Constitution directed that:
> ". . . at the general election to be held in the year one thousand nine hundred and sixteen, and every twentieth year thereafter, and also at such times as the Legislature may by law provide, the question: 'Shall there be a convention to revise the Constitution and amend the same?' shall be decided by the electors

of the state" (New York, *Constitution* [1894] art. 14, sec. 2, ed. Francis N. Thorpe, *The Federal and State Constitutions*, 7 vols. [Washington: Government Printing Office, 1909] 5:2735).

The provision for twenty year intervals was a carryover from the 1846 Constitution (New York, *Constitution* [1846], art. 13, sec. 2, ed. Benjamin P. Poore, *The Federal and State Constitutions*, 2 vols. [Washington: Government Printing Office, 1878] 2:1366) and was popular with many states. Harvey C. Mansfield has suggested that it can be traced to Jefferson's well known remark, "God forbid, that we should ever be twenty years without a revolution" (Harvey C. Mansfield, "The States in the American System," *The Forty-Eight States* [The Eighth American Assembly, 1955], p. 46).

³Of its 175 members, 98 were "at least nominally Republicans" (Frank Hamlin, "New York Constitutional Convention," *Yale Law Journal* 4 [June 1895]: 214).

⁴Over the protests of the Democrats, the Republican majority had inserted a provision into the Constitution which prevented any one county in the state from having more than one third of all State Senators, and any two adjoining counties from having more than half, regardless of their populations (New York, *Constitution* [1894], art. 3, sec. 4, ed. Francis N. Thorpe, 5:2703). This provision was obviously aimed at such densely populated, and overwhelmingly Democratic, New York City counties as Kings (Brooklyn) and New York.

⁵This was recognized by such contemporary observers of New York State politics as Charles A. Beard (Charles A. Beard, "The New York Constitutional Convention," *National Municipal Review* 4 [October 1915]:637) and Walter T. Arndt (Walter T. Arndt, "The Defeated New York Constitution," *National Municipal Review* 5 [January 1916]:94).

⁶Edgar C. Murlin, *The New York Red Book* (Albany: J. B. Lyon Co., 1914), p. 665; and Ibid., (1915), p. 716.

⁷Ibid. Even this margin was brought into question as some voters brought suit in the summer of 1914 against what they claimed were voting irregularities in the twelfth and fourteenth Assembly Districts in New York City. Eventually the allegation was dismissed in court, but the taint remained. For a fuller discussion of this see J. Hampden Dougherty, *Constitutional History of the State of New York*, 2nd ed. (New York: Neale, 1915), pp. 377-379.

⁸For the definitive study of the Sulzer impeachment see Jacob A. Friedman, *The Impeachment of Governor William Sulzer* (New York: Columbia University Press, 1939).

⁹Ibid., pp. 259-261.

¹⁰Ray B. Smith, ed., *History of the State of New York, Political and Governmental*, 6 vols. (Syracuse, The Syracuse Press Inc., 1922), vol. 4: *History of The State of New York, Political and Governmental, 1896-1920*, by Roscoe C. E. Brown, p. 259.

¹¹The fact that they had at least won approval of a convention, by however small a margin, could not be considered a significant victory. In the past, the voters had approved a constitutional convention each time the question of holding one had been put to them (Frances D. Lyon, "New York State Constitutional Conventions," *New York State History* 20 [New York State Historical Association, January 1939]:51).

¹²John Lord O'Brian, *The Reminiscences of John Lord O'Brian* (New York: Columbia University Oral History Research Office, 1952), p. 140.

¹³By provision of the 1894 constitution, constitutional conventions were to be composed of three delegates from each Senatorial district, of which there were, in 1915, fifty-one and fifteen delegates at large (New York, *Constitution* [1894], art. 14, sec. 2, ed. Francis N. Thorpe, 5:2735).

¹⁴Warren Moscow, *The Last of the Big Time Bosses* (New York: Stein & Day, Publishers, 1971), p. 14.

¹⁵These figures were provided by George A. Blauvelt, "The Work of the Constitutional Convention," *Cornell Law Quarterly* 1 (November 1915):19.

¹⁶Elihu Root to John Lord O'Brian, February 11, 1915, Elihu Root Papers, U.S. Library of Congress, Washington, D.C.; and Frederick C. Wadhams, Secretary of

New York State Bar Association, to Henry L. Stimson, January 15, 1915; Henry L. Stimson Papers, Yale University, New Haven, CT.

[17]Blauvelt, p. 19.

[18]Undated item in Frederick C. Tanner Papers, Columbia University, New York, N.Y.

[19]G. G. Benjamin, "The Attempted Revision of the State Constitution of New York," *American Political Science Review* 1 (February 1916):25.

[20]In the constitutional conventions of 1821 and 1846 the office of the secretary of state distributed questionnaires to the delegates which asked, among other things, the delegates' occupations (Lyon, p. 54). No similar measure was taken at the 1915 convention. However, two delegates to the Convention did record the occupations of their fellow delegates. George A. Blauvelt offered this breakdown: "Lawyers, 125; Publicists, 7; Educators, 4; Bankers, 4; Physicians, 2; Architects, 1; and Miscellaneous, 25" (Blauvelt, p. 19). Frederick C. Tanners' breakdown differs only slightly: "Lawyers, 126; Newspapermen and editors, 6; College Presidents, 3; Professors, 1; Businessmen, 10; Bankers, 4; Architects, 1; Traders, 3; Florists, 2; Manufacturers, 3; Real Estate and Insurance, 5; Civil Engineers, 1; Court reporters, 1; and Doctors, 2" (undated item in Frederick C. Tanner Papers).

[21]Jacob Gould Schurman, "The New Constitution for the State of New York," *The Cornell Law Quarterly* 1 (November 1915):17.

[22]O'Brian, p. 140.

[23]Frederick C. Tanner, *The Oral History of Frederick C. Tanner*, 2 vols. (New York: Columbia University Oral history Research Office, 1950) 1:140.

[24]Stanley Isaacs, *The Reminiscences of Stanley Isaacs*, 2 vols. (New York: Columbia University Oral History Research Office, 1950), 1:29.

[25]William Barnes to Elihu Root, April 10, 1915, Elihu Root Papers.

[26]James Bryce, *The American Commonwealth*, 2 vols. (New York: The MacMillan Co., 1893; reprint ed., 1912) 1:458; and Henry J. Ford, "The Reorganization of State Government," *Proceedings of the Academy of Political Science* 3 (New York, January 1913:78.

[27]For a discussion of the beginnings of such preparation by the states see Walter F. Dodd, "The Constitutional Convention: Preliminary Work, Procedure and Submission of Conclusions," *Proceedings of the Academy of Political Science* 5 (New York, October 1914):54-57.

[28]Ibid., p. 55.

[29]Ibid., p. 56.

[30]New York, *Laws* (1914), chapter 261.

[31]Ibid.

[32]Albert L. Sturm, *Methods of State Constitutional Reform* (Ann Arbor: University of Michigan Press, 1954), p. 109.

[33]Ibid., p. 163.

[34]New York, *Laws* (1913), chapter 280.

[35]New York State Department of Efficiency and Economy, *Government of the State of New York; A Survey of its Organization and Functions* (Albany: J. B. Lyon Co., Printers, 1915), p. xi. For the definitive study of the bureau's early work in the period 1906-1921, including an account of its cooperation with the Department of Efficiency and Economy, to which the account presented here is indebted, see Jane S. Dahlberg, *The New York Bureau of Municipal Research, Pioneer in Government Administration* (New York: New York University Press, 1966).

[36]N.Y.S. Dept. of Efficiency and Economy, p. vii.

[37]For examples of these see earlier discussion, pp. 14-15.

[38]N.Y.S. Dept. of Efficiency and Economy, p. vii.

[39]Quoted in Dahlberg p. 45.

[40]For a full discussion of the bureau's philosophy see Ibid., pp. 31-50.

[41]New York Bureau of Municipal Research, "The Constitution and Government of the State of New York: An Appraisal," *Municipal Research*, no. 61, (May 1915).

[42]Most of the actual writing was, according to Luther Gulick, Beard's work.

(Interview with Dr. Luther Gulick, New York, N.Y., November 13, 1974.)
[43]N.Y. Bureau of Municipal Research, p. 2.
[44]Ibid.
[45]See earlier discussion, pp. 14-15.
[46]N.Y. Bureau of Municipal Research, p. 5.
[47]Ibid., p. 81.
[48]Ibid., p. 96.
[49]Indeed, the "Appraisal," together with the other materials provided to the Convention by the Bureau, became, in Ferrel Heady's words, ". . . a primer for the administrative reorganization movement . . ." as a whole (Ferrel Heady, *State Constitutions: The Structure of Administration* [New York: National Municipal League, 1961], p. 3).
[50]N.Y. Bureau of Municipal Research, p. 1.
[51]These included copies of amendments introduced in the legislature over the previous ten years, a digest of all the state constitutions, and descriptive reports on city governments.
[52]Henry L. Stimson to Charles Evans Hughes, November 21, 1910, Henry L. Stimson Papers.
[53]Elting E. Morison, *Turmoil and Tradition: A Study of the Life and Times of Henry L. Stimson* (Boston: Houghton Mifflin Co., 1960), p. 216.
[54]McGeorge Bundy and Henry L. Stimson, *On Active Service in Peace and War* (New York: Harper, 1948), pp. 56-62.
[55]Ibid., pp. 57-58.
[56]Ibid., p. 58.
[57]Henry L. Stimson, "Some Phases of the Progressive Movement in the Republican Party," address delivered at the McKinley Day Banquet of the Tippecanoe Club of Cleveland, Ohio. A copy of this speech can be found in the Henry L. Stimson Papers.
[58]Though, to be sure, Stimson's second point was essentially, if not explicitly, an argument for a short ballot. On other occasions Stimson was quite explicit in his support of a short ballot. This was especially true during his gubernatorial campaign, which began with a statement that included the following line: ". . . one of the greatest reforms of the future lies along the lines of the so-called 'Short-Ballot' system" (acceptance of Republican nomination speech, October 4, 1910, Henry L. Stimson Papers).
[59]McGeorge Bundy and Henry L. Stimson, p. 58.
[60]He could hardly have been unaware of this as the mail-reaction to his Cleveland address included negative as well as positive responses. A particularly severe negative reaction, which was a portent of their clash later in the convention over the same issue, was received by Stimson from prominent upstate Republican, Edgar T. Brackett (see Henry L. Stimson to Edgar T. Brackett, February 9, 1911, Henry L. Stimson Papers).
[61]Henry L. Stimson to James B. Reynolds, February 9, 1911, Henry L. Stimson Papers.
[62]O'Brian, p. 175.
[63]Jacob Gould Schurman to Elon Brown, May 5, 1914, Elihu Root Papers.
[64]James W. Wadsworth, *The Reminiscences of James W. Wadsworth*, 3 vols. (New York: Columbia University Oral History Research Office, 1951) 1:95.
[65]Ibid., p. 98.
[66]Hamlin, p. 215.
[67]Bernard B. Steiner recalled this statement by Stimson in a letter to him on May 1, 1913, Henry L. Stimson Papers.
[68]Morison, p. 69.
[69]Ibid., p. 95.
[70]Later, of course, Stimson was to occupy still another high post previously held by Root, that of secretary of state in the Hoover Administration (1929-1933).

[71]Phillip C. Jessup, *Elihu Root*, 2 vols. (New York: Dodd Mead and Co., 1938) 2:290.

[72]Neither Root's papers nor Stimson's provides any clue as to just how or when this occurred.

[73]Jessup, 2:290-291.

[74]Elon Brown to Henry L. Stimson, May 12, 1914, Henry L. Stimson Papers.

[75]Stimson mentioned this in three letters he wrote on the fourteenth of June (Henry L. Stimson to Harold J. Hinman, John Lord O'Brian, and Charles M. Hamilton, June 14, 1914, Henry L. Stimson Papers).

[76]There is no mention of names he might have recommended in either Root's or Stimson's papers.

[77]Henry L. Stimson to Elihu Root, June 5, 1914, Henry L. Stimson Papers.

[78]Henry L. Stimson, "Responsible Government, A Republican Constitutional Program," *The Independent*, July 6, 1914, pp. 14-16.

[79]Edgar T. Brackett to Henry L. Stimson, July 16, 1914, Henry L. Stimson Papers.

[80]Ibid., July 28, 1914.

[81]Alphonse T. Clearwater to Henry L. Stimson, July 18, 1914, Henry L. Stimson Papers.

[82]Jacob Gould Schurman to Henry L. Stimson, July 17, 1914, Henry L. Stimson Papers.

[83]Seth Low to Henry L. Stimson, July 14, 1914, Henry L. Stimson Papers.

[84]Henry L. Stimson to Frederick C. Tanner, June 13, 1914, Frederick C. Tanner Papers.

[85]Henry L. Stimson to Cornelia C. Bryce, August 4, 1914, Henry L. Stimson Papers. Stimson also made substantially the same point in a letter to Edgar Dawson on August 10, 1914 (Henry L. Stimson Papers).

[86]This he revealed in a letter to Cleveland Runyon on June 3, 1914 (Henry L. Stimson Papers).

[87]By this time the committee was no longer, strictly speaking, a Committee of Twenty-five. At Stimson's request (Henry L. Stimson to Elihu Root, June 5, 1914, Henry L. Stimson Papers), Root had appointed several additional persons to the committee. Just how many there now were is difficult to determine. Seth Low referred at one time to "twenty-eight" members (undated item in Seth Low Papers, Columbia University, New York, N.Y.). On two occasions Stimson referred to "thirty" (Henry L. Stimson to Elihu Root, July 20, 1914, Henry L. Stimson Papers; and Henry L. Stimson to Clinton Rogers Woodruff, July 22, 1914, Henry L. Stimson Papers). Herbert Parsons' minutes of the meeting on the twenty-fourth of July referred to "thirty-one" (undated item in Herbert Parsons Papers, Columbia University, New York, N.Y.). And John Lord O'Brian would later recall a total of "thirty-nine" members (O'Brian, p. 136). In all probability the different figures reflect the growth of the committee over the period of time up to the July meeting and shortly thereafter.

[88]The eight were: Alphonse T. Clearwater, William D. Guthrie, Darwin R. James, Seth Low, Phillip J. McCook, John Lord O'Brian, Jacob Gould Schurman, and Ralph W. Thomas.

[89]This was almost certainly the case with Seth Low who had written to Stimson and suggested that he be made a member of the committee (Seth Low to Henry L. Stimson, June 2, 1914, Henry L. Stimson Papers).

[90]Henry L. Stimson to Elihu Root, June 5, 1914, Henry L. Stimson Papers.

[91]O'Brian, p. 138.

[92]Henry L. Stimson to Elihu Root, August 6, 1914, Henry L. Stimson Papers.

[93]*Draft of Platform in Matter of Constitutional Amendments, Submitted to the Committee of Thirty by the Sub-committee of Nine Appointed for that Purpose* (New York: The Evening Post Job Printing Office, August 1914).

[94]Significantly, it did not use the term "executive budget." Perhaps this was a concession to Guthrie and the one or two allies he may have had on the subcommittee. A better explanation might be that Stimson was looking ahead to the reaction of

the full committee and decided to go slowly, merely recommending a budget at first and then, having secured approval of the budget principle, pressing for an executive budget in the constitutional convention. Another interesting point is that Stimson left out two of the three main recommendations of his 1911 Cleveland address—namely a lengthened term of office and a more powerful legislative role for the governor. There, too, he may have been concerned about making his recommendations palatable to the whole committee and decided to drop these two for the present. Whatever the reason, it is apparent that by this time Stimson's priorities lay in the area of the three traditional recommendations of the reorganization movement.

[95]*Proceedings of the Republican State Convention Held at Saratoga Springs, New York, August 18, 19, 1914,* (New York: Published under the supervision of the Secretary of the Convention, Republican State Committee, 1914), p. 95.

[96]Elihu Root to Henry L. Stimson, August 4, 1914, Elihu Root Papers.

[97]*Proceedings of the Republican State Convention,* p. 107.

[98]Henry L. Stimson to Richard S. Childs, December 4, 1914, Henry L. Stimson Papers.

[99]Henry L. Stimson to Herbert S. Houston, December 31, 1914; to Albert S. Bard, January 9, 1915; to William H. Taft, January 11, 1915; and to S. Sidney B. Roby, March 9, 1915, Henry L. Stimson Papers.

[100]This does not mean, of course, that he ceased all activity on behalf of reorganization, rather, that whatever limited activities he did engage in were less visible to the public. One example of this was his involvement in an address by former President William H. Taft to the State Bar Association on January 22, 1915. On learning that Taft was scheduled to speak on the subject of the upcoming constitutional convention, Stimson addressed letters to Taft and Elihu Root. To Taft he wrote of the importance of reorganization, the opportunity of the convention to do something about it, and the role of the Republican party:

"I have a very high conception of the importance of this convention. It comes at a psychological moment when the country, tired with the foolish and half-baked attempts to cure admitted evils in state government by remedies which would only make these evils worse, are turning to the Republican Party for help."

He concluded by urging Taft to endorse the reorganization recommendations of the party platform, in his address (Henry L. Stimson to William H. Taft, January 11, 1915, Henry L. Stimson Papers). Of Root, Stimson requested that he too write Taft and urge him to say something positive about reorganization (Henry L. Stimson to Elihu Root, January 11, 1915, Henry L. Stimson Papers). Taft, whose advocacy of reorganization on the federal level, especially regarding an executive budget, was well-known, replied immediately in the affirmative (William H. Taft to Henry L. Stimson, January 12, 1915, Henry L. Stimson Papers). After Taft's address, in which he strongly endorsed reorganization, Stimson made certain that copies of the speech reached delegates to the convention (Henry L. Stimson to William H. Taft, January 26, 1915, Henry L. Stimson Papers.).

[101]Charles H. Young to Herbert Parsons, October 16, 1914, Herbert Parsons Papers. This lack of public awareness and interest was the result of not only the fact that the convention was called for reasons of narrow, partisan politics and not in order to decide pressing or controversial matters (see earlier discussion, p. 36), but also because the European war tended, quite naturally, to drain public attention away from anything else—Elihu Root was not the only one whose thoughts were preoccupied with the war.

[102]See earlier discussion, pp. 35-41.

Chapter 3

The Convention

The earliest activities of a constitutional convention—selecting a convention president, assigning the delegates to committees and designating committee chairmen—are always of importance to the success of any measure with which the convention will deal. In the case of reorganization and the 1915 convention, these activities were of critical importance. It is difficult to exaggerate the influence that selection of a president and committee chairmen, and committee assignments had on the manner in which the convention addressed the issue of reorganization.

SELECTION OF A PRESIDENT

The first order of business when the convention assembled in Albany on April 6 was the selection of a president. Not that there was much doubt as to who the choice would be. Given the 64-vote edge held by the Republicans, it was obvious that it would be a Republican. And given that fact, it was clear that the choice would be Elihu Root. His stature was such that Republicans would automatically look to him for leadership, and his experience and ability were so abundant that he was more than qualified for the post, as his biographer wrote:

> His eminence in party circles, his intellectual power, his past and present official positions and the fact that he had been second in command at the Constitutional Convention of 1894, made his choice not only inevitable but eminently suitable.[1]

71

In fact, well before the convention met there had been some movement among key delegates to ensure that the position would be Root's. On December 24, 1914, Herbert Parsons wrote to Seth Low informing him of a meeting he had had with Stimson in which the two agreed to back Root for the presidency and to urge others to do the same. Assuming Low was of the same mind, Parsons concluded by asking if Low would undertake to contact all the Republican delegates, advising them that his choice for president, and that of Stimson and Parsons, was Root, and asking them whom they preferred for the post. It would be most appropriate for Low to take such an initiative, wrote Parsons, as it was he who had received the most votes for delegate at large.[2] Low promptly agreed to do as requested and proceeded to send letters to the Republican delegates.

The idea behind these letters was twofold. First, they would make known to the delegates the choice of three eminent Republicans which would, presumably, influence their own choice. Second, in the event there were delegates whose preference was for someone other than Root, their responses to Low's letter would identify them early on and allow Low, Parsons, and Stimson time to attempt to change their minds before the convention. As it happened, few minds, if any, needed to be changed. The results of Low's canvass were overwhelmingly favorable to Root. On December 31, Stimson, who had been in touch with many Republican delegates in this period, wrote: "I have yet to find any Republican who did not propose to vote for Mr. Root. . . ."[3] Root's election was thus quite predictable and few were surprised when he won by a vote of 133 to 32 against Democrat Morgan J. O'Brien, in a vote divided almost entirely along party lines.

Root's election was an important victory for reorganization. For while he was a relatively recent convert to reorganization, Root had become, under Stimson's tutelage, one of its most enthusiastic and vocal champions and was looking forward to having the convention give reorganization its highest priority. This is evident from two of his major pre-convention pronouncements. On November 19, 1914, he addressed the Academy of Political Science on the subject of the upcoming convention. Referring to the work the convention would undertake, Root spoke only in the most general terms, except for one item, reorganization. On the need for a "practical overhauling of the machinery of state government"[4] he spoke explicitly, forcefully, and at relative length. Then on March 25, 1915, in an address to the Merchants Association of New York, he again made specific mention of reorganization alone as an appropriate area of work for the convention and added the principles upon which the reorganization should take place:

> . . . there is one thing which the convention, I feel, ought to do. The business of government in this state, and in most of our states, has outgrown the machinery; or many of our states, I will say, have outgrown the machinery of government. . . .

> . . . the time clearly has come when the machinery of government shall be reformed so that it shall be competent to attend to the business. We are running a railroad with a stage-coach organization.

> The first thing—the one all-important thing—is to make the organization so that responsibility shall be fixed. You and I don't know who is really responsible in our state government for what goes wrong or for what goes right. We don't know who really are to be blamed, and we don't know who really ought to be praised; and there is no way of having effective service in government any more than in a business enterprise unless you can put your finger on the man who is responsible for this error, or should be commended for that success.

> And in order that there shall be responsibility, power must go with the responsibility. You cannot hold men responsible unless you give them power. The Governor of the state today is being unjustly criticised for not doing things that our system withholds the power to do from him, and that will be so until we have improved the system on business principles.[5]

The degree of Root's commitment to reorganization should thus have been known to all before the convention opened. But if there were still some doubts, they were immediately laid to rest by his opening remarks to the convention. In his Presidential acceptance speech, in words that echoed his previous pronouncements, Root declared that:

> The most obvious duty before us is to scrutinize attentively the framework of the state government in order to ascertain in what respect, if any, the established institutions are insufficient or ill-adapted to accomplish the ends of government. Great changes have come in the industrial and social life of the state since the last convention. . . . The business which government is required to undertake has vastly increased both in magnitude and variety and there is a widespread feeling that in some respects the business of the government has outgrown the organization of government. . . .

> The fundamental principle to be applied I take to be that responsibility and power shall always go together. Responsibility without power can never be justly enforced, and power without responsibility can never be duly controlled.[6]

Though it did not dwell on specifics, Root's address also made reference to the necessity of a short ballot and a consolidation of administrative agencies. In this way did Root make his commitment to reorganization, in both its general principles and its particulars, unmistakably clear to the convention from the outset.

As president, Root would hold considerable influence over the convention, and the occasions on which he could make use of this influence on behalf of reorganization would be numerous. The first such opportunity, and the occasion on which he used his influence most effectively, was the division of the delegates into committees and the designation of committee chairmen. These tasks fell, of course, to the president, and it was here that Root made his first contribution to reorganization in the convention.

COMMITTEE ASSIGNMENTS

On the second day of the convention, Root called a recess of some three weeks in order to enable him to work on committee assignments. On the same day, he wrote to all the delegates, asking them on which of the 30 committees they wished to serve. Their preferences would be taken into consideration, he indicated, but by no means would he be bound by them. For one thing, too many delegates might ask for the same committee assignments,[7] and too few for some other assignments. For another, Root had his own ideas as to which delegates ought to serve on which committees. In large part, these ideas were based on the delegates' varied talents and experience. They were also based, however, on the delegates' sympathies and attitudes towards the subject matter with which the various committees were likely to deal. In the case of his selections for the two committees which would deal with reorganization measures—the committee on the governor and other state officers, which would work on a short ballot and a consolidation of administrative agencies, and the committee on state finances, which would work on an executive budget—it was this last factor which weighed most heavily.

Root knew that if reorganization measures were to be considered by the convention, much less approved, they would first have to meet with the approval of these two committees. Thus, it was important that the delegates assigned to these committees be sympathetic to reorganization. To help him in selecting two such groups, Root turned to his close friend and fellow reorganization advocate, Stimson. As a result of his pre-convention work for reorganization, Stimson knew where many of the delegates stood on the issue. On other delegates, of whose position he was less sure, Stimson made discreet inquiries and reported his findings to

Root.[8] With Stimson's help,[9] Root fashioned two 17-member groups of whose receptivity to reorganization he could be reasonably certain. Needless to say, Stimson was appointed to both groups.[10]

Having named the membership of the committee on the governor and other state officers and the committee on state finances, Root turned to the easier task of appointing their respective chairmen. One of the two posts would, of course, go to Stimson, and while there is no record of his having actually been offered a choice by Root, it is safe to assume that either position would have been his for the asking. That he chose state finances may be explained by the fact that although Stimson was equally dedicated to a short ballot, consolidation of agencies, and an executive budget, it was only in the area of budgeting that he had had some practical experience, albeit limited, during his tenure as secretary of war. His two years in the War Department confirmed in actual experience what he had accepted on an intellectual level about the need for an executive budget, as he observed in his autobiography:

> The particular importance of the executive budget had come home to Stimson during his years in the War Department, where he had been forced to study at firsthand the consequences of haphazard financial methods. He there discovered that routine War Department appropriations were in the hands of seven different committees and subcommittees of Congress and that the authority of the Secretary of War in controlling expenditures in his own Department was negligible.[11]

It was thus understandable that having to choose between working in two equally important areas, he chose the area on which he could bring to bear some firsthand experience. For the chairmanship of the committee on the governor and other state officers, Root picked Frederick C. Tanner, New York City delegate at large and, since October 1914, Republican state chairman. Tanner had asked for the position[12] and Root, aware of both Tanner's favorable attitude toward reorganization[13] and his prominent party position, was only too happy to accommodate him.

Root's selections for the committees which would deal with reorganization measures would contribute directly to the success of reorganization in the convention. The nature of the membership ensured that such measures would reach the convention floor and the prestige of the chairmen provided reorganization with influential spokesmen. There was, however, another selection which Root made in this period which would make a less direct, though equally important, contribution. This was his selection of George W. Wickersham for the chairmanship of the committee on the judiciary. By itself, this position had little to do with the reorganization issue and the question of who occupied it would have been of little consequence to reorganization's fortunes. What was important was the fact that it traditionally carried with it the post of convention floor leader. This made it the number two position in the convention as a whole and gave it a role in all the major questions facing the convention. That it would be held by Wickersham, a supporter of reorganization who had served on the Taft Commission and was a trustee of the New York Bureau of Municipal Research, would be of great help when the convention took up the question of reorganization. But the significance of Root's selection of Wickersham lay in more than the fact that another reorganization supporter had been chosen for a position of influence in the convention. It also lay in who Root might have appointed and did not.

From the start, there had been pressure on Root to appoint Edgar T. Brackett chairman of the judiciary committee. Brackett wanted the position[14] and he was the favorite of his fellow upstate Republicans who argued that his experience in this area was unmatched by any other delegate. Brackett had, in fact, been a member of the state Senate judiciary committee for 11 years, eight of them as chairman, and the case for him was a strong one. Nevertheless, Root resisted these pressures and chose Wickersham.

It is, of course, possible that Root's decision was motivated by a variety of factors and not just by the implications this decision held for reorganization. But it is certain that the impact this decision would have on reorganization was a prime motivating factor. Brackett had, after all, been a leader of the anti-reorganization group in the party's pre-convention preparations and he would undoubtedly play a similar role in the convention. The last thing Root wanted to do was to hand him the position which carried with it the influential post of floor leader.

Brackett took Root's decision very hard. In fact, it may well be that his opposition to Root throughout the convention, over reorganization as well as other issues, might not have been as harsh or as personal as it was after this rejection. John Lord O'Brian suggested this connection when he recalled that "when Brackett was left out and Wickersham put in, that was a personal affront that Brackett never got over until he died" and that as a result, "[Brackett] lost no opportunity throughout the convention of saying snide things about [Root and his supporters]."[15] Given his adamant pre-convention opposition to reorganization, however, it is quite certain that he would not have yielded on the substance of the issue at all in any event. Thus, on balance, it was clearly a victory for reorganization when he was denied this important convention post.[16]

Root's rejection of Brackett for the chairmanship of judiciary and, thus, the position of floor leader, was made even more significant by an incident which took place in this period involving former State Chairman William Barnes. Barnes, a delegate and a leader of the conservative upstate Republicans who had, together with Brackett, argued strenuously at the state convention of the previous summer against approval of reorganization planks for the party platform, was expected to join with Brackett in leading the assault on reorganization in the convention.[17]

However, the opening days of the convention found him with his mind and much of his energy not on convention related work but on a law suit he was pursuing in Syracuse against former President Theodore Roosevelt. Roosevelt, who had been a bitter enemy of Barnes ever since the 1912 Republican national convention, when the latter had been instrumental in the decision of the convention to deny him the Presidential nomination, had charged Barnes with collusion with Tammany boss Charles Murphy in certain corrupt dealings. This prompted Barnes to bring a libel suit against Roosevelt. When the case was decided on May 22 in favor of Roosevelt, the effect on Barnes was enormous. Personally, he was crushed. "I am tired to the heart. I could lie down and wish never to get up,"[18] he was heard to remark to a fellow convention delegate on his way home. Politically, he lost much prestige.

The result was that he had no taste for involving himself in the convention's work and that his influence, even where he sought to use it, was much diminished. A contemporary observer characterized him as "astonishingly meek and mild" in the convention and attributed this condition to his "recent disastrous joust with Mr. Theodore Roosevelt."[19] And a delegate, Frederick C. Tanner, recalling Barnes' role in the convention, stated: "I think that he was discounted so far as his work in the Convention was concerned, and his influence in it was also lessened to a very great degree, because of the impact of this libel suit."[20] With Barnes neutralized, the leadership of the anti-reorganization forces in the convention fell to Brackett. As a result of Root's action, however, Brackett was in a poor position to offer it.

The impact of Root's actions in this early period of committee assignments on the success of reorganization in the convention was evident throughout the work of the convention. This is especially true of the convention's first stage, committee work.

COMMITTEE WORK

Root announced the membership of the committees on April 26, and from that day through much of the month of July the convention labored in committees. Each measure introduced on the convention floor was referred to the appropriate committees which proceeded to study its merits in one, two, and sometimes three-a-day sessions. From the outset, the committe on state finances (hereinafter referred to as the Stimson committee) and the committee on the governor and other state officers (hereinafter referred to as the Tanner committee) worked closely together. It was the common objective of Stimson and Tanner to produce amendments which would complement one another in a comprehensive reorganization of the state government. To this end, they paid close attention to the work of each other's committees, arranged to hear many of the same witnesses, and, on some occasions, conducted joint hearings.[21]

A total of 70[22] different proposed amendments were referred to the Tanner committee. In the course of its deliberations on these proposals, the committee heard some seventy witnesses, including former State Commissioner of Efficiency and Economy John H. Delaney,[23] and the following state officials: comptroller, treasurer, engineer, superintendent of public works, commissioner of highways, chairman of the tax commission, commissioner of education, commissioner of excise, and commissioner of agriculture. The Stimson committee had 44 amendments referred to it. In its deliberations it heard from, among others, New York City Comptroller William H. Prendergast; former Governor and State Comptroller Martin Glynn; Syracuse Mayor Fobes; and Congressman John J. Fitzgerald, chairman of the House appropriations committee. Some of the witnesses gave testimony pertaining to amendments before the committees, while others spoke in a general way on the committees' work. Whether they spoke generally or with reference to a specific amendment, the great majority favored reorganization and urged adoption of a short ballot, a consolidation of administrative agencies, and an executive budget.

This, of course, was not surprising. As chairmen, Stimson and Tanner played the key roles in deciding who would address their respective committees, and, while they invited a few reorganization foes, such as upstate Senator Elon Brown, for "balance," they saw to it that the bulk of the testimony would back reorganization. Moreover, they saw to it that those who testified in favor of reorganization would be men of considerable prestige whose opinions would carry weight with the members of the committees and the convention members generally. For the most prominent of

these witnesses, they arranged joint hearings of the two committees. The joint hearing accommodated these prominent citizens
who might be inconvenienced by having to appear on two separate
occasions. More importantly they also provided them with a more
dramatic and attention grabbing forum in which to express their
pro-reorganization sentiments.

The highpoint of the hearings conducted by the two committees
were the joint hearings. Appearing before them were such outstanding public figures as former President William H. Taft, U.S.
Senator James W. Wadsworth from New York, President Frank J.
Goodnow of Johns Hopkins University, and President A. Lawrence
Lowell of Harvard University, all of whom urged reorganization in
the most forceful terms. Also invited to appear before a joint
hearing was another prominent individual who had been identified
with state reorganization and who would surely have lent his
support to reorganization in his testimony, President Woodrow
Wilson. Wilson responded that much as he would like to journey to
Albany, the press of business relating to the European war—the
sinking of the Lusitania in which 124 Americans lost their lives
occurred on May 7—prevented him from doing so.[24]

Stimson and Tanner also thought of inviting former President
Theodore Roosevelt to testify. They were certain of his support of
reorganization and were intrigued with the idea of presenting both
Taft and Roosevelt, bitter political enemies who were at odds over
most other issues, as advocates of reorganization. On reflection,
however, they decided not to invite Roosevelt. An invitation at this
time might be resented by Barnes and his supporters who were still
smarting over Barnes' loss in his recent altercation with Roosevelt,
and they could not afford to alienate any delegates whose support
they would be seeking for reorganization.[25]

Stimson and Tanner planned the joint hearings carefully. Not
only were they selective in their choice of witnesses so as to ensure
that the greater weight of the testimony would be favorable to
reorganization, they also orchestrated the order of appearances of
the witnesses in order to maximize their contribution to the
reorganization effort. Thus, they saved their most distinguished
witness, Taft, for near the end, building up to his appearance by
having relatively less distinguished individuals precede him. Stimson acknowledged as much in his letter inviting Taft to appear.
Observing that Goodnow would be appearing the first week in
June, he asked Taft: "Could you come up the following week? to
put the capstone on our edifice?"[26] Combined with the stature of
the witnesses, the effect of this careful planning was to make the

joint hearings an impressive series of demonstrations on behalf of reorganization.

Favorable to reorganization as they were, it cannot be said with certainty that the hearings would have in themselves swayed a confirmed opponent of reorganization. Rather, they served to reinforce the opinions of those who leaned toward reorganization, and to help those who sincerely questioned its merits to arrive at a positive conclusion. Thanks to Root's selections for the two committees, however, this was, at most, all that was needed in order to secure the committees' approval of reorganization amendments. In fact, shortly after the hearings began, it became evident that the question was not whether the committees would approve reorganization amendments, but what specific features these amendments would include.

A short ballot could be, in Charles A. Beard's words, "... short, shorter, or shortest."[27] It could leave as elective positions only those of the governor and lieutenant governor, or could extend to the comptroller and attorney general, or to some few other officers. Similarly, a consolidation of administrative agencies could be accomplished within a large number of different organizational schemes. As to an executive budget, here, too, questions of detail had to be confronted. These questions involved not only the specific procedures to be used in formulating the budget, but what powers the legislature could exercise upon receiving the budget. It was these questions of detail the committees had to address.

The committees' answers to these questions were not long in coming. On June eighth, ninth, and tenth, State Senator, and delegate, John G. Saxe introduced reorganization amendments on the convention floor, which had been drafted by the New York Bureau of Municipal Research and were based on the principles enunciated in its "Appraisal." After a second reading, the amendments were referred to the Stimson and Tanner committees. Then, on June 24, Saxe and Frederick A. Cleveland of the bureau came before the committees to explain the amendments. Their presentation was well received. The Saxe amendments fit Stimson's and Tanner's conception of reorganization and appealed to most of the other members as well. Following a period of debate and discussion over the next few weeks, the committees agreed on two reorganization amendments almost identical to those proposed by the bureau and Saxe.

One amendment, produced by the Stimson committee, prescribed an executive budget for the state. The amendment directed the heads of all executive departments to submit to the governor on or before November 15 of each year itemized estimates of the monies they would require for the ensuing fiscal year. Upon receiving the estimates, the governor would hold public hearings and, based on the input these hearings provided and his own judgment, make appropriate revisions. On or before the following February, the governor would submit to the legislature a budget consisting of a comprehensive plan of proposed expenditures and estimated revenues.

The budget would be accompanied by a statement of the current assets and liabilities, and surplus or deficit of the state; an estimate of its financial condition as of the beginning and end of the ensuing fiscal year; and a statement of revenues and expenditures for the two fiscal years immediately preceding the ensuing fiscal year, in such form as to be suitable for comparison. The budget would also be accompanied by proposed appropriation bills. The governor, comptroller, and the heads of the departments would have the right to appear before either house of the legislature to explain or defend aspects of the budget, and they would be obligated to do so if asked to by either house.[28]

The legislature's budgetary power would be limited to striking out or reducing items in the budget; under no circumstances would it be permitted to increase the size of any proposed appropriations. Furthermore, no appropriation bills would be entertained by either house until those proposed by the governor were acted upon by both houses. Finally, appropriation bills proposed by the governor would become law immediately upon approval by the legislature, without any further action required of the governor.

The other amendment, produced by the Tanner committee, provided for a short ballot and a consolidation of administrative agencies. Under the amendment, the only state positions to remain elective would be those of the governor, lieutenant governor, comptroller, and the attorney general. The comptroller would head a Department of Audit and Control, and the attorney general, a Department of Justice. In addition to these two departments, there would be 13 others, the heads of which, with but a single exception, would be appointed by the governor with the advice and consent of the Senate.[29] All of the prevailing departments, offices, boards, and commissions would be subsumed under one or another of these 15 central departments. The amendment left it to the legislature to review the nature and function of the many state agencies and assign them to the appropriate departments. However, the amendment clearly prohibited the legislature, as well as the governor, from creating additional departments.

The Stimson committee reported out its amendment first on August 4. Together with the amendment, the committee sent to the convention a report written by Stimson. The report was at once an eloquent statement of the case for an executive budget and a clever propaganda piece designed to win support for the amendment. It began by describing the rapid and continuing increase in state government expenditures and the lack of a corollary rise in population and revenue sources,[30] all of which made it imperative for the state to use sound financial methods in conducting its business. It then went on to argue that the prevailing system was anything but sound.

A major defect in the system was that it made no provision for responsible executive revisions of agency estimates. That is, that each of the many agencies—and here the report alluded to the disorganized multiplicity of agencies and the need for consolidation—decided on its own how much it would require, and sent its requests directly to the legislature. The legislature was thus the recipient of large numbers of requests which were made without regard to one another. The result was that it had to balance the competing requests by making revisions. But it was in a poor position to do so. For one thing, argued the report,

> ... [the legislature] has no administrative control or authority over the bureaus and departments through which the moneys [sic] of the state are expended. . . . It is therefore without the consistent regular information as to operating difficulties, problems, methods and costs. . . . Instead, it must act upon such information as it can acquire through hearings held by committees, meeting only occasionally.[31]

Secondly, "the legislature cannot exercise executive supervision to compel a given bureau to try to produce the desired result with less money by adopting a more efficient method."[32] For these reasons, concluded the report, the legislature was not the appropriate body to make revisions of agency estimates.

A more fundamental defect in the system, however, went beyond the question of the legislature's fitness to make revisions of agency estimates to the larger issue of whether the legislature ought to be the focal point in the preparation of the state's financial plan of expenditure. The report argued that it should not. One reason was the legislature's orientation:

> The legislature is under the disadvantage that its members, instead of being responsible solely to the state as a whole, are each responsible to and dependent upon a single district of the state. A financial program, made up in the first instance by the legislature, necessarily tends to represent a compromise or bargain between different districts, rather than the viewpoint of the state as a whole.[33]

A plan of expenditure formulated by the legislature was thus not necessarily in the best interests of the state as a whole. A second reason the legislature ought not to be the focal point in the preparation of the plan of expenditure, was that such an arrangement, while seemingly expressive of the legislature's power, actually eroded its historic function of holding the purse strings of the state, and, in effect, reversed the appropriate relationship of the executive to the legislature:

> The present system presents a singular reversal of the proper relation which should maintain between the executive and the legislators. Instead of the executive coming to the legislature with a request for funds, which it is the province of the legislature to pass upon and either grant or refuse, our system has gradually resulted in the legislature presenting to the excutive appropriation bills. . . . Instead of the man who is to spend the money presenting to the body which is to grant the money his requests for their final decision, the latter body, in substance, draw their check in blank and present it to the executive for him to determine how much of it he cares to use.[34]

The report also faulted the prevailing system in that it did not provide for a comprehensive financial plan for the state. The legislature responded to the separate agency requests in a series of separate appropriations. At no time during the process was a clear overview had, or even sought, of the overall expenditures of the state. Certainly, there was no attempt made to relate proposed expenditures to estimated revenues and to the general financial condition of the state. This, asserted the report, was irresponsible.

The report went on to present the committee's recommendations, or the particulars of its amendment, and to point out that each of the objectionable aspects of the prevailing system would be rectified by the system envisioned by the amendment. It concluded with a brief summary of possible arguments that might be made against the amendment and appropriate refutations.[35]

The Tanner committee reported out its amendment on August 11, and it too was accompanied by a report written by the chairman. Tanner's report, however, was different from that of Stimson's. It was a much shorter and less detailed statement whose general aim was not so much to win support for the committee's amendment— as was the aim of the Stimson report with its systematic presentation of arguments for an executive budget—as to simply assert its positions and to explain its recommndations.

The basic position was summed up in this statement:

> The present constitution, Article IV, Section 4, provides that the governor "shall take care that the laws are faithfully executed." It is the opinion of your committee that the executive machinery placed at

his disposal is not well suited to the purpose, and makes economy and efficiency in the administration of such laws practically impossible.[36]

To buttress this assertion, the report described the tangled mass of state agencies and the arbitrariness of the system which designated some positions as elective and others, of equivalent stature, as appointive. It then offered its own succinct explanation for this state of affairs: "The existing plan of state government is not a creation by design, but is a growth by accretion."[37] If the system was to be improved, argued the report, it would have to be restructured according to a careful design. And it was just such a design, based on the twin cornerstones of a short ballot and consolidation of agencies, that the committee's amendment provided. The report then went on to explain the amendment.[38]

In addition to Tanner's report, two important minority reports were filed by committee members Courtlandt Nicoll and Arthur J. Baldwin. Both reports took exception to the amendment's short ballot provision; Nicoll arguing that it did not go far enough, and Baldwin submitting that any shortening of the ballot was undemocratic. Nicoll believed that the logic of the short ballot idea demanded that only the highest positions, those of governor and lieutenant governor, be left elective, an argument with which Stimson and Tanner wrestled prior to rejecting, and which will be treated, along with their reason for rejecting it, shortly. Baldwin, on the other hand, considered the short ballot idea itself inappropriate in a democracy. His report was the first official statement of the anti-reorganization forces in the convention[39] and it echoed the argument used by Brackett and his allies in the Republican preconvention activities:

> I dissent from this so-called "Short Ballot Bill." However admirable the purpose, the means suggested are fallacious. The cure is worse than the ill. Centralized government might tend to economy, but it would inevitably bring discontent, and discontent destroys the mental poise of democracy. Popular government may not work for economy, but that is not sufficient reason for its destruction.

> If the convention believe that oligarchy is better than democracy, let us be frank and tell the truth, and not deceive the people with a sugar-coated catch phrase. This plan would enthrone one man. . . . It would give such power as would have gladdened the heart of Alexander, the tyrant of Pheroe, or satiated the cupidity of that modern dictator, Castro of Venezuela. Pure democracy, with its direct ballot, is impossible with 10,000,000 of people. Its opposite, an aristocracy or monarchy, is contrary to all our traditions. Our fathers gave us a middle course, representative government. To this let us

cling. The constitution is the embodiment of the experience of the past. It needs repose, not change.[40]

The reporting out of amendments and the filing of reports closed out the first stage of the convention's work. Excepting the discordant note struck by Baldwin's report, this first stage had gone entirely to the satisfaction of the reorganization advocates. As has been indicated, this was not unexpected, given the fact that the members of the two committees were largely handpicked for their receptivity to reorganization. Far less predictable was the second stage, consideration by the full convention of the amendments. The Baldwin report, while a singular voice in the committees, was surely representative of the views of others in the convention. And they would be no less vehement in their opposition to aspects of the amendments during the convention debates. Nevertheless, there were some factors operating in favor of reorganization which, on the whole, made the outlook for reorganization on the eve of the debates a positive one.

Prospects for Reorganization on the Eve of the Debates

First and foremost of the factors operating in favor of reorganization was the fact that reorganization measures had been overwhelmingly approved by two convention committees. The committees had been officially charged with investigating the question of reorganization on behalf of the convention and they had arrived at their conclusions after much discussion and study. It was only reasonable to expect that their conclusions would now be accorded the serious consideration, if not the immediate acceptance, of the convention. This would have been the case even if those conclusions would have presented the convention with completely new ideas. In fact, recommendations for reorganization were, of course, not new to the members. They had all been recipients, through the constitutional convention commission, of the bureau's "Appraisal," and they were aware of the Republican party platform's commitment to reorganization in the convention. The committees' recommendations were thus in concurrence with, and gave specific expression to, what had already been recommended to the convention by others. This gave their recommendations the advantage of a cumulative effect.

Another important favorable factor was the power and prestige of the reorganization advocate's leadership—Root, Stimson, Tanner, and Wickersham. That reorganization had gotten this far in the convention was largely due to Root's influence.[41] Now he would use his influence to secure the approval of the full convention. Helping him to do so would be floor leader Wickersham, and Stimson and Tanner, who, as chairmen of the two committees, would lead the fight for reorganization on the convention floor. They, too, would make use of their considerable influence among the Republican members.

A third favorable factor was the fact that the reorganization amendments approved by the committees were not as radical as they might have been. The executive budget covered only expenditures for state administrative purposes, leaving out local, pork-barrel appropriations, which would remain in the hands of the legislature. Stimson and the other architects of the executive budget were aware of the abuses which took place in these appropriations and of the need for reforms, but they were also aware of how important they were to the legislators and that any changes in this area would evoke tremendous opposition to the new budget system. For this reason they compromised, as Beard wrote shortly after the convention:

> [That the executive budget did not eliminate the abuses of pork-barrel appropriations] was not overlooked at the time of the passage of the amendment, but it was doubtless believed to be inexpedient to disturb too violently the time-honored methods for the distribution of public plunder.[42]

Another item on which the reorganizers compromised was the short ballot. Reorganizers had long been united in their demands for the shortening of the ballot to include none but the two highest offices in the state. Yet, the amendment reported out of committee extended it to the comptroller and attorney general. Here again, the reason was to make the amendment as palatable as could be to as large a number of people as possible.[43] Lest this be thought an insignificant compromise, it should be pointed out that it occasioned great controversy among the reorganization advocates and brought a great deal of criticism down on Stimson's head.[44] Replying to this criticism, Stimson wrote, in a letter to Richard S. Childs, of the need to be realistic:

> I have, however, been studying closely the temper of the Convention. . . . The psychology of the members is peculiar. They are conservative men of substance, and they resent being told, however truthfully, that either they or their constituents need a shorter ballot. . . . I think we shall accomplish substantial reform in the direction of efficiency and concentration of responsibility but we shall not succeed in making all of the state officers appointive. . . . Do not be dis-

appointed if [this] seems less than you expected.There will be substantial advances in my opinion, and in view of the conservative tem-
per of the Convention I hope we will have cause for mutual con-
gratulation.[45]

Having put forward less radical reorganization amendments than
they might have, the reorganization advocates could expect a
greater receptivity to reorganization in the full convention.

A fourth, and last, favorable factor was the attitude of the
Democrats to the work of the convention. Outnumbered as they
were, the Democrats had long before the opening of the convention
given up all hope of accomplishing the one objective they had
sought when they began their agitation for a constitutional convention, a rewriting of the constitution's apportionment provision. It
would not have been surprising therefore, had they adopted an
attitude of indifference or even partisan obstructionism to the work
of the convention.

Much to the satisfaction of the Republicans, the Democrats chose
instead to take an active part in the convention on a largely
nonpartisan basis. That they did so may well have been due to Root.
As the number two man in the 1894 convention, Root had deplored
the fact that it had been run on strictly party lines,[46] and he was
determined not to repeat that experience in 1915. To this end, he
consulted at length with such Democratic leaders as Morgan J.
O'Brien and Delancey Nicoll on committee assignments for the
Democrats, took care not to favor one party over the other in his
Presidential decisions,[47] and constantly emphasized, in public and
in private, the necessity for nonpartisanship in the activities of the
convention.[48] Apparently the Democrats reacted in kind.

One result of this nonpartisan atmosphere was that it permitted
those Democrats who favored reorganization or who seriously
considered it, to react positively to the Root-Stimson-Tanner program and not to reject it automatically as a Republican, and
therefore unworthy, plan. Thus, the amendments approved by the
Stimson and Tanner committees were approved by a majority of
the Democrats as well as the Republicans on the committees. This
encouraged Republican reorganization advocates like Stimson,
who had long been laboring on behalf of reorganization among
Republicans exclusively, to look to the possibility of Democratic
support in the full convention.

These were the factors which favored reorganization on the eve
of the convention debates. They did not, of course, guarantee
reorganization's success, but they very much enhanced its chances.
And if the reorganization advocates could not assume with certainty

that they would be successful, they could at least proceed to the debates with a degree of optimism.

THE DEBATES: THE EXECUTIVE BUDGET

The Stimson committee's amendment, having been reported out before that of the Tanner Committee, was taken up first by the convention, on August 10. This circumstance would prove fortuitous for reorganization. For of the two amendments, the executive budget was the less objectionable to reorganization foes, and the momentum created by the relatively easy passage of the first reorganization amendment would carry over to the debate over the second. The reason that the executive budget was less objectionable lay in one of the key arguments used by Stimson. As we have seen, the case for the executive budget, as framed by Stimson, was that in addition to promoting responsible government, it would restore the proper relationship between the executive and the legislature. It would do this by returning control of the public purse to the legislature where it belonged; putting the onus of formulating the financial plan of expenditure on the governor, which he would then be obliged to defend to the legislature, and leaving the decision to grant or withhold approval of the plan to the legislature.

This argument spoke to the fears of those who were suspicious of reorganization because of their concern with maintaining the prerogatives of the legislature and preventing the accumulation of too much power by the governor.[49] It allayed their fears by pointing out that far from yielding power to the governor, the legislature, under the executive budget system, assumed a more authoritative position in the budgetary process. That the argument was a cogent one is evident from the course of the debate on the executive budget.

The debate began with an opening address by Stimson. The address, which took some three hours, was essentially a review of and an expansion on his report to the convention. As in the report, but at greater length, he cited: the constantly increasing expenditures of the state, asserting that the rate of increase was higher in New York than in any other state,[50] and the consequent need for sound financial methods; the lack of a comprehensive financial plan under the prevailing system; the lack of attention to the needs of the state as a whole; and what he called the "shifting of functions,"[51] or reversed roles, of the governor and the legislature. All these, he went on to explain, would be resolved by adoption of the executive budget. Throughout his talk, he stressed above all that, despite the fact that under the executive budget it would be the governor and not the legislature who would initiate the financial plan, this would not make for an increase in the power of the governor at the expense of the legislature, arguing that:

> . . . [the executive budget] confers no additional power upon the Governor over what he has today. To-day he has the right to veto any appropriation which is passed by the Legislature. He has the final say. All that this plan does, so far as his power is concerned, is to transfer the exercise of that power to the beginning of the performance and to compel him to make his proposals in public, to lay his hands on the table, to submit them to the scrutiny that will come during the legislative session. . . .
>
> The only thing it takes from the legislature—the only duty that it takes from the legislature is the administrative duty of making a financial plan. . . . And to say that to take that out of the hands of the legislature is to impair its dignity and power is like telling the doctor that when he seeks to keep poison out of the stomach he is an enemy of the stomach and is seeking to destroy its dignity and function. On the contrary, gentlemen the purpose of this is not to destroy, but to recreate legislative dignity and power, to place our legislative body in a condition where they will be able to devote themselves intelligently to the consideration of the broad fiscal policies of this state upon which they will have the final decision. . . . If to remove from them that function is to destroy their dignity and their power, I very much misunderstand what dignity and power is.[52]

To gain the support of those delegates who might remain unmoved by his arguments, he invoked such authorities as Lord Bryce, former Governor and Comptroller Martin Glynn, and Senator James W. Wadsworth to support one or another of his points, and emphasized repeatedly that the committee's conclusions "were reached only after very long and careful consideration [and] the compromise of different views,"[53] and that those conclusions were supported "by a substantially unanimous vote"[54] in the committee. These appeals for support on the basis of endorsements by distinguished public figures and the committee members, combined with his substantive arguments to make the address a persuasive presentation on behalf of the executive budget.[55]

That Stimson's address was effective and that the executive budget would carry, were immediately apparent from the ensuing debate. The focus of this debate was largely not on whether the amendment was too radical a measure, but rather on whether it went far enough. Specifically, some delegates found fault with the aforementioned compromise by Stimson which limited the budget to state administrative purposes and provided no reforms in the area of local, pork-barrel appropriations.[56] Other delegates thought

Stimson's concession to the legislature in that it could demand that the governor appear to answer questions relating to the budget was an unnecessary infringement on the authority, and a blow to the dignity, of the governor. Given the thrust of these criticisms—that the amendment was actually less revolutionary than what was hoped for—and given the fact that it was criticisms of this nature and relevant discussion which formed much of the debate, it was clear to all that the amendment would be approved by the convention.[57] This included Stimson's chief antagonist over the executive budget, and over reorganization generally, Edgar T. Brackett. When Brackett rose to argue against the executive budget, in the only anti-budget address of any substantial length or force to be delivered in the convention, he began by acknowledging that it would undoubtedly be approved.[58]

Indeed, Brackett explained that he would not have ventured to speak out on the issue at all, were it not for the fact that the criticisms of the prevailing system voiced by Stimson and others were overly harsh on the legislature:

> I should not, Mr. Chairman, care to take the time of this Committee or to say a word on the subject if it were not for the fact that I have noticed, from the beginning of the discussion clear through, on one side a continued jeremiad toward the Legislature of the State. And I find that in the criticism of the action of the Legislature of the State, it is hoped to find the chief reason why this change should be made.[59]

It was, thus, primarily in defense of the legislature that he rose to speak. And this he proceeded to do:

> Why, gentlemen, . . . I would think as I sat here, from some criticisms that are made by members who have spoken here, that the system of the State has been a mere bedlam; . . . that the members of the Legislature have come down here each year, and, like drunken sailors, have simply dipped their hands deep into the treasury of the State and thrown the proceeds far and wide, without rhyme or reason.
>
> Mr. Chairman, it pleased a kind Providence to give me the honor of serving in the Legislature of the State of New York fifteen long, hard-working years. It will be the pride and delight of my last years, however long it may please the good Lord to leave me here, to know that it was my privilege to serve for that great length of time with the unselfish, the devoted, the industrious, the noble men who, in the main, made up that body. Does the distinguished chairman of this Committee think that the appropriations of this State for a great many years have been made without the most painstaking saving and care? . . . I bear cheerful witness that while there were things that went through the successive Legislatures of which I did not approve, that while there were many things which the wisdom of time has demonstrated were not best, they were scrutinized with painstaking care

and with the honorable intention to do exact justice to the people of
the State, and for the persons for whom the appropriations were
made, and that, instead of having been squandered, it was with the
most painstaking parsimony that the sums were doled out.[60]

Having defended the integrity of the legislature, Brackett then
continued to a denunciation of the executive budget. The focus of
his attack was the narrow fact that it would take a long-standing
function of the legislature, that of initiating the financial plan, and
give it to the governor. This could only be interpreted, he argued,
as an increase in the power of the governor and a decrease in that of
the legislature. As such, the executive budget was nothing less than
a step toward autocracy:

> . . . you have taken the first step, I care not how small it is, away from
> representative government and toward an autocracy. It may be small,
> it may, Mr. Chairman, be hardly perceptible, but the next step is
> easier. We have accustomed the coming generation to getting away
> from the true standards, and while it may be after you and I, Mr.
> Chairman, have become forgotten dust, but just as surely as the time
> shall come, it will prove that the departure from self-government, that
> the surrender of self-government, the surrender that will come in
> favor of autocracy, will be found to have had its root in the departure
> that we may make here from representative government and from the
> true conception of the legislative function.[61]

Obviously, Brackett was not impressed with Stimson's argument
that despite the change in the initiating function, the executive
budget would, on the whole, enhance the position of the legislature.[62] But the overwhelming majority of the delegates must have
been impressed, for when Brackett completed his argument, concluding with the dramatic statement: "Therefore, Mr. Chairman,
calling attention to the fact that the legislature is being destroyed, I
shall simply content myself hereafter by voting yes or no. . . ,"[63] he
received very little support from anyone. And when the final vote
was taken, a total of only three votes joined Brackett's in opposition
to the executive budget.[64]

The vote on the first reorganization amendment was heartening
to the reorganization advocates. Not only was the executive budget
approved almost unanimously, but it was approved in the same
form as it had come out of committee. Moreover, while the easy
passage of the first amendment in no way implied convention
approval of the second, it did generate, as was noted earlier, a
certain amount of pro-reorganization momentum which would be
helpful in the debate over the second amendment.

THE DEBATES: THE SHORT BALLOT
AND CONSOLIDATION OF AGENCIES

The debate on the second reorganization amendment, begun on August 27, was lengthy, intense and emotion filled.[65] One reason for its length was the fact that there was, inevitably, a great deal of repetition in the arguments put forth by the various delegates on both sides of the issue. For this reason the focus here will be on the chief spokesmen for both sides. It was their arguments which were most often used by the other delegates, and it was upon their presentations that the two sides ultimately rested their respective cases.

The main body of the debate dealt with the short ballot. The principal argument of the reorganization foes was that reorganization was undemocratic, and the short ballot, which would reduce the number of popularly filled offices and grant, instead, greater appointing powers to one man, was particularly vulnerable to this charge. Consequently, they concentrated their efforts on this aspect of the amendment. In response, the reorganization advocates spent the bulk of their time defending the short ballot.

The initial presentations on behalf of the short ballot were made by Tanner and Wickersham. Their basic argument was the importance of responsible government and the difficulty of fixing responsibility in a system characterized by divided and overlapping executive powers, an argument by now familiar to the delegates from their reading of the "Appraisal" and succinctly summed up in this statement by Tanner:

> The most important thing in constituting government is to unite responsibility with power, so that a certain known person may be definitely responsible for doing what ought to be done, be rewarded if he does it, and punished if he does not do it, and that the person held responsible shall have the power to do the thing. Under our system we have divided the executive power among many separately elected heads of departments; and we have thus obscured responsibility, because of the complicated affairs of our government, it is hard for the best informed to know who is to be blamed or who is to be praised, who ought to be rewarded, or who punished.[66]

The short ballot, they submitted, resolved this problem by concentrating power and responsibility in the governor. In addition to this well-known argument, they appealed to the Republican delegates on the basis of a hitherto unmentioned argument. This was that since the 1914 Republican party platform advocated a short ballot, they were constrained to support one. Tanner conceded that the platform explicitly stated that it would not obligate individual

Republican delegates to vote in accordance with any of its provisions, but contended nevertheless that "true" party men could not ignore the official party position on the issue. To proclaim one's allegiance to party and then disregard official party policy was nothing but "hypocrisy!"[67]

The reply to these arguments, and the case against the short ballot, came in an address by Brackett.[68] The thrust of his remarks, that the short ballot was undemocratic and a step towards autocracy, was, of course, entirely predictable. But the eloquence with which Brackett articulated his position gave it new life and force. He began by framing the issue as he saw it:

> I believe the present juncture to be a pivotal one in the State of New York. I believe that the question whether we shall continue to be a democracy or shall turn our faces against democracy is involved in the discussion which we are here having. It is clearly only upon us to decide here and now whether we shall continue in its breadth and in its strength and in its integrity the system of manhood suffrage under which we have traveled for three-quarters of a century, or whether, the most reactionary of reactionaries, we shall turn back the hands of our political clock seventy years and return to a system that was then recognized as outgrown and as unfitting for a free people. There is truly involved here, stated briefly and succinctly, the question whether the great State of New York shall to-day turn her back on the progress in self-government, and turn her face toward the past and to the Russian idea.[69]

He then proceeded to present his position on the issue:

> There has recently sprung up a . . . demand for what is known as the short ballot. . . . Where it came from I do not know . . . but I am sure that, whatever its source and whoever its sponsor, it came from a heart that in its inmost core hates self-government and that seeks for opportunity to limit and curtail it. It was conceived in the malignancy of one who despises the control by the people of their own affairs, and it was born in that spirit of aristocracy that seeks to limit participation in actual government to as small a percentage of the electorate as possible. . . . Try all that you may; disguise as you can; honey the pill all that is possible, it still stands and everyone who takes the trouble to think about it must know that it stands true, that the plan is projected in fear of the results of elections by the people and in a wish to get as far away from such results, of election by the people, as possible. It may be supported by some so delighted with any change as to embrace any new thing proposed, but it was conceived by some cunning mind, which hated real Democracy, the rule of the people, the possessor of which believed he had found a way to take a step away from it.

> . . . Now, do not, I pray you, think that I am hysterical. I am not foolish enough to believe that the fact that the Governor of the State of New York is allowed to name the Secretary of State and . . . the other

officers named, will create any government cataclysm. The structure of government will remain. The public work will be carried on. The records will be written in down [sic] in the Secretary of State's office just as before. There will be no immediate shaking of the foundations. But you have taken a step away from the true doctrine of a republic and in the direction of the quagmires that have enveloped every previous attempt in that direction. Your coming generation, brought up in toleration of the situation reached by this false step, brought up in toleration of the theory that all State officers should be appointed, will presently tolerate the next step, the appointment of the judiciary, and then the next step, the appointment of your county officers, and presently you have your "man on horseback" and your absolute government. You have taken a step in the wrong direction. The coming generation will be less quick to discern and check the next false step and the succeeding steps to absolutism will succeed with frightful rapidity. . . . I would to God I could impress on you that we must pass the heritage along as we received it; that we must give it as it came to us, unhampered and unfettered by restraints; that the only true principle is to give the people direct and immediate control of their officers, that they be permitted to elect as many of them as may be; that their terms shall be short; that we continue as we received our heritage of government, with freedom's soil beneath our feet and freedom's banner waving o'er us.[70]

Brackett did not respond to the argument of responsible government directly, but implicit in his remarks was the response that no argument, however meritorious, justified approval of an undemocratic proposal. As to the argument that the Republican platform constrained him to support a short ballot, Brackett reminded the delegates that this section of the platform had been approved by the state convention at the urging of a Committee of Twenty-five. This committee, he charged, was totally unrepresentative of the rank and file party membership and was weighted from the outset in favor of reorganization.[71] The platform's endorsement of a short ballot was thus not a true expression of the way the Republican party, as a whole, felt about the issue, and Republicans need not be bound by it.

 Brackett also called into question the credentials of the reorganization advocates' leadership. First, he made the point that their experience was, in the main, executive experience. He specifically mentioned: Root, who had been a secretary of war and secretary of state; Stimson, who had been a secretary of war and United States attorney; and Wickersham, who had been a United States attorney general. These men, he asserted, could not speak objectively about proposals which added to the power of the executive. They would be inclined to favor expansions of executive power even at the expense of democratic government. Furthermore, he pointed out that they had worked primarily in Washington and therefore had, he argued, little knowledge of the state's problems and needs. For these men, to whom he referred collectively as "the Federal crowd," to return to the state and offer their hastily formed judgments on state government reform, was an act of arrogance:

> Most of you have been engaged outside of the State. You have been down in Washington. You have been learning things in a different sphere, and when you come back into the State, we let you get up on the seat alongside of us and we are driving along, trying to give you a lift and help you along on a long and dusty road, and then after a few minutes you reach over and take the lines and say, "We will attend to this, we know more about the affairs of the State than you people who have been living here and been studying it for years."[72]

Brackett's forceful and lengthy address provoked responses from numbers of prominent pro-reorganization delegates, among them, Stimson, Low, Delancey Nicoll, and, in the climax of the debate, Root. These responses argued that Brackett's view of the short ballot was the product of an unthinking conservatism which feared the slightest reform, and that far from the imagined problems Brackett warned against, the real and immediate problem the state had to be concerned with was irresponsible government. In the two most effective responses, Nicoll stressed the former point, while Root emphasized the latter.

Nicoll, one of the older Democrats and a leading attorney, was an outstanding speaker with a gift for sarcasm and ridicule. Much to the delight of the other reorganization advocates, he now turned his talents on Brackett. Asserting that the short ballot was "not, after all is said . . . very radical,"[73] he continued in mock amazement:

> And yet, gentlemen, the most remarkable part of this discussion . . . is that although this amendment goes such a very little way, it has excited the most intense antagonism on the part of the delegate from . . . Saratoga, whose oration of . . . Saturday afternoon, denounced us all, Democrats and Republicans alike, as being engaged in a conspiracy to steal away the liberties of the people and establish an autocratic and oligarchic form of government. He said because we were going to adopt this little measure of reform . . . that we were actually pulling the whole temple down and striking a blow at the very foundation of our Republican system. Ah, I must say to my dear old Cincinnatus from Saratoga, the old order of things gives place to the new and we of the next generation must listen to the music of progress and keep step with the march of events. If this amendment shall pass . . . I want to say this to my old and venerable friend from Saratoga: Content yourself with the motto of Cato to his son: "When vice prevails and impious men bear sway the post of honor is a

private station." Retire, sir, retire, sir, to the green pastures and the
still waters of your beloved farm and, removed from the pomps and
vanities of this wicked world and all the sinful lusts of the flesh,
devote the remainder of your days to the cultivation of its fertile soil,
your hand never off the plow, except when you whip up the old horse,
and your eyes never off the furrows except when you lift them to
Heaven . . . after the day is over, call around you by the old stove the
little people of the hills and tell them the sad and harrowing tale of
this Convention: How you came here with the determination to
protect the peoples' rights, and like old Pigstyles in Parliament, raise
the devil with everything and everybody, and how you were defeated
in your patriotic endeavors by the machinations of the people's
enemies and by a gross betrayal on the part of those on whom you
counted as friends, and then, sir, wearied with your virtuous labors,
wrap your mantle—wrap your shirt around you, and lie down to
pleasant dreams, dreaming of a heaven where they have elections
everyday, where even the doorkeeper in the House of the Lord is
elected, where no man is ever appointed to office, where all ballots
are long and all terms are short, where only the spirits of the Old
Guard that never surrenders are admitted and where the souls of the
ungodly federal crowd are stopped at the gate.[74]

Whether these words affected the delegates' thinking on the short
ballot is unclear, but one thing is certain—they had a devastating
effect on Brackett himself. John Lord O'Brian recalled that "the
ridicule excited by that one speech practically put Brackett out of
action for the rest of the Convention."[75] Thus, if Nicoll's address
did not win over any individual delegates, it still contributed
substantially to the short ballot cause by striking at the opposition's
leadership and rendering it less active.

An even more effective reply to Brackett was made by Root. Root
almost never took the floor throughout the convention, preferring
instead to stay aloof from the debates in a proper bipartisan
presidential role. In the case of the short ballot, however, he made
an exception, and gave his reason for doing so at the outset of his
remarks:

I have had great doubts as to whether or not I should impose any
remarks on this bill upon the Convention . . . but I have been so long
deeply interested in the subject of this bill, and I shall have so few
opportunities hereafter, perhaps never another, that I cannot refrain
from testifying to my faith upon the principles of government which
underlie the measure that is before us, and putting upon this record
for whatever it may be worth the conclusion, which I have reached
upon the teachings of long experience in many positions, through
many years of participation in the public affairs of this State and in
observation of them.[76]

Having thus explained his participation in the debate, Root
proceeded to a defense of the short ballot. Essentially his argument

was that rather than the short ballot being undemocratic, it was the prevailing system with its long ballot that was truly undemocratic. For the principal element in a democratic republic was the responsibility, the answerability, of the elected officials to the people. And, owing to the division of power in the executive which clouded individual responsibility, it was precisely this element which was missing in the prevailing system.

Now, this lack of responsibility was, by itself, sufficient reason to question the democracy of the prevailing system. There was, however, another factor which compounded the problem. This was the fact that a certain kind of responsibility on the part of the elected official did exist under the system. Not, to be sure, to the people, but to a small segment of the people. This segment consisted of those people who had helped engineer the official's election—the party bosses. It was to them that the official felt beholden and, lacking a responsibility to anyone else, it was only to them that he felt responsible. Thus it was that a system which did not ensure responsibility to the people resulted in a government which was the very antithesis of a democracy. That is, a government not by the many, but by a powerful few.

Root's argument was, of course, not a new one. The reorganization advocates had, as we have seen, long argued that the lack of clear responsibility in government fostered the growth and health of "invisible government." What was different about Root's presentation was that he did not make this argument merely on a theoretical level, but spoke bluntly about the situation in New York State; declaring that "invisible government" had reigned in the state for years and asserting that it had its roots in the state's irresponsible system of divided executive powers:

> I am going to discuss a subject now that goes back to the beginning of the political life of the oldest man in this Convention, and one to which we cannot close our eyes, if we keep the obligations of our oath. We talk about the government of the Constitution. We have spent many days in discussing the powers of this and that and the other officer. What is the government of this State? What has it been during the forty years of my acquaintance with it? . . . From the days of Fenton, and Conklin, and Arthur and Cornell, and Platt, from the days of David B. Hill, down to the present time the government of the State has presented two different lines of activity, one of the constitutional and statutory officers of the State, and the other of the party leaders—they call them party bosses. They call the system—I don't coin the phrase, I adopt it because it carries its own meaning—the system they call "invisible government" for I don't remember how many years Mr. Conklin was the supreme ruler in this State, the Governor did not count, the legislatures did not count; comptrollers

and secretaries of state and what not, did not count. It was what Mr. Conklin said, and in a great outburst of public rage he was pulled down. Then Mr. Platt ruled the State; for nigh upon twenty years he ruled it. It was not the Governor; it was not the Legislature; it was not any elected officers; it was Mr. Platt. And the capitol was not here; it was at 49 Broadway; Mr. Platt and his lieutenants. It makes no difference what name you give, whether you call it Fenton or Conklin or Cornell or Arthur or Platt, or by the names of men now living. The ruler of the State during the greater part of the forty years of my acquaintance with the State government has not been any man authorized by the Constitution or by the law, and, sir, there is throughout the length and width of this State a deep and sullen and long-continued resentment at being governed thus by men not of the people's choosing. . . .

Mr. Chairman, that system finds its opportunity in the division of powers, in a six-headed executive, in which, by the natural workings of human nature there shall be opposition and discord and the playing of one force against the other, and so, when we refuse to make one governor elected by the people the real chief executive, we make inevitable the setting up of a chief executive not selected by the people, not acting for the people's interest, but for the selfish interest of the few who control the party, whichever party it may be.[77]

Root's argument appealed to the delegates' reason. But he did not, in his address, appeal to their reason alone. For, in addition to presenting a rational argument, the address played on the emotions of the delegates. It stressed that the chance to vote for the short ballot was a once in a lifetime opportunity, and that, as such, should be viewed as a singular privilege. It emphasized that a vote for the short ballot would give the delegates' children and grandchildren just cause to be proud. It even managed to tie in the European war and to invoke God's name:

Mr. Chairman, this Convention is a great event in the life of every man in this room. A body which sits but once in twenty years to deal with the fundamental law of the State deals not only for the present but for the future, not only by its results but by its example. Opportunity knocks at the door of every man in this assemblage, an opportunity which will never come again to most of us. While millions of men are fighting and dying for their countries across the ocean, while government is become serious, sober, almost alarming in its effect upon the happiness of the lives of all that are dearest to us, it is our inestimable privilege to do something here in moving our beloved State along the pathway towards better and purer government, a more pervasive morality and a more effective exercise of the powers of government which preserves the liberty of the people. When you go back to your homes and review the record of the summer, you will find in it cause for your children and your children's children, who will review the Convention of 1915 as we have been reviewing the work of the preceding Conventions, to say, my father, my grandfather, helped to do this work for our State. Mr. Chairman, there is a plain old house in the hills of Oneida, overlooking the valley of the Mohawk, where truth and honor dwelt in my youth. When I go back, as I am about to go, to spend my declining years, I mean to go with the feeling that I can say I have not failed to speak and to act in accordance with the lessons that I learned there from the God of my fathers. God grant that this opportunity for service to our country and our State may not be neglected by any of the men for whom I feel so deep a friendship in this Convention.[78]

The address had a powerful effect on the convention. To some extent, this was due to Root's status as convention president and Republican party elder statesman, and would, therefore, have been the case almost regardless of the content of the address. But it is quite clear that the address itself had also moved the convention, and that it had done so because of its emotional content. Emotionalism was out of character for Root, whose public demeanor was almost always cool—many said icy—and detached.[79] His emotionalism over the short ballot was, therefore, bound to impress his listeners. And it did. John Lord O'Brian recalled the address this way:

> I shall never forget the effect [the address] had on the convention. Root always spoke very deliberately and quietly, even when he was deeply moved, but there was a tone in his voice that was very penetrating that came out when he got stirred up. I remember old Jim Wadsworth . . . sitting beside me that day with tears running down his cheeks as Root recalled the past and begged these delegates to consider the moral needs of the time in terms of government.[80]

And Richard S. Childs remembered the scene at the conclusion of the address: "The convention immediately broke into disorder; everybody streamed out to the lobby to talk about this sensational event."[81]

The conclusion of Root's address marked the end, for a practical matter, of the debate on the short ballot. While some discussion on the subject continued for a short time, the principal speakers had spoken and the main arguments had been made.[82] Now all that remained was the vote. Its outcome was not difficult to predict. The aforementioned factors favorable to reorganization on the eve of the debates—including the respect normally accorded committee recommendations, the influence of the reorganization advocates' leadership, the relatively less radical nature of the reorganization amendments, and the cooperation of the Democrats—and the momentum generated by the easy passage of the first amendment, had put the reorganization foes at a distinct disadvantage at the outset of the debate on the second amendment.

For them, it was essential that a strong case be made against the short ballot in the debate. To some extent, this had been done by Brackett. But the combination of the Nicoll and Root speeches had, at the least, served to blunt whatever effect Brackett's address had had. There was little doubt, in the wake of Root's address, that the short ballot, and the second amendment, would carry. The only remaining question was what the margin would be. The answer to that came on September 2, one day after the Root address, when the second reorganization amendment passed by a vote of 125 to 30.[83]

REORGANIZATION'S SUCCESS:
A SIGNIFICANT BUT PRELIMINARY VICTORY

The convention passed on the reorganization amendments, though not on them alone, once more before it adjourned. On September 10, at its last session, the convention voted on the newly revised constitution, consisting of the old constitution and the 33 amendments it had approved, in its entirety. In a vote strikingly similar to the one on the second reorganization amendment, the convention approved the new constitution 118 to 33. The vote marked the official victory of reorganization in the convention.

The reorganization advocates took a great deal of justifiable pride in their victory. They had succeeded in making New York "the first state that has ever undertaken to frame the financial measures of its consitution around the budget idea."[84] They had provided for the first large scale reorganization of a state administrative system. And they had significantly shortened the state ballot.[85] Collectively, these reforms, in the words of Beard, "[made] possible the establishment of a degree of responsible government hitherto unknown in American politics,"[86] and, in Wickersham's words, they "placed the Empire State as the first one of the American commonwealths to deal intelligently, scientifically and courageously with this vast, complicated, inartistic, unscientific expensive, wasteful system of government that has grown up in our midst."[87]

Proud of their achievement as they were, and significant an achievement as it was, the reorganization advocates recognized that the convention's approval did not constitute final victory. This could only come upon ratification by the electorate of the amendments. By decision of the convention, the 33 amendments would not be submitted to the voters separately or in small groups. Rather, the great bulk of them, including the two dealing with reorganization, would be put to the voters in one, all or nothing proposition. This was of no concern to the reorganization advocates. The reorganization amendments were by far the most controversial, and whether they were presented to the voters apart from the other amendments or together with them, it was reorganization which would be the overriding issue in the campaign for ratification.[88] The task of the reorganization advocates was to mount the strongest possible campaign for reorganization. With the adjournment of the convention, this is what they set about to do.

NOTES

[1]Phillip C. Jessup, *Elihu Root*, 2 vols. (New York: Dodd Mead and Co. 1938), 2:292.

[2]Herbert Parsons to Seth Low, December 24, 1914, Henry L. Stimson Papers, Yale University, New Haven, CT.

[3]Henry L. Stimson to Israel T. Deyo, December 31, 1914, Henry L. Stimson Papers.

[4]Elihu Root, "The Principles and Practice of Constitutional Revision," address delivered to the Academy of Political Science, November 19, 1914, in *Addresses on Government and Citizenship* (Cambridge: Harvard University Press, 1916), p. 151.

[5]Idem, "The Business Men and the Constitutional Convention," address delivered to the Merchants Association of New York, March 25, 1915, in *Addresses*, pp. 160-161.

[6]New York State Constitutional Convention, 1915, *Revised Record of the Constitutional Convention of the State of New York, 1915*, 4 vols. (Albany: J. B. Lyon Co., Printers, 1915), 1:11-12.

[7]This is precisely what happened in the case of the Committee on the Judiciary. Two days after he sent out the letters, Root complained that there were "too many eminent lawyers clamoring for the place [membership on the Judiciary Committee]" (Elihu Root to N.V.V. Franchot, April 9, 1915, Elihu Root Papers, U.S. Library of Congress, Washington, D.C.).

[8]See Sidney B. Roby to Henry L. Stimson, April 16, 1915, and Henry L. Stimson to Sidney B. Roby April 26, 1915, Henry L. Stimson Papers.

[9]Root consulted at least one other prominent reorganization advocate. This was Richard S. Childs, whom he asked for names of delegates who would support a short ballot, for appointment to the Committee on the Governor and Other State Officers (Richard S. Childs, *The Reminiscences of Richard S. Childs* [New York: Columbia University Oral History Research Office, 1950], p. 6.

[10]The other members of the Committee on the Governor and Other State Officers were: Frederick C. Tanner, Rush Rhees, Edward N. Smith, Patrick W. Cullinan, Ledyard P. Hale, Edward E. Franchot, George L. Bockes, Courtlandt Nicoll, Robert S. Pelletreau, Edward M. Angell, William R. Bayes, George A. Blauvelt, William N. Dykman, Arthur J. Baldwin, Francis Martin, and James F. Donnelly. On the Committee on State Finances, in addition to Stimson, were: Harold J. Hinman, Seth Low, Robert S. Pelletreau, Herbert Parsons, Leroy A. Lincoln, Frank R. Lennox, Seward H. Van Ness, H. Leroy Austin, Samuel H. Beach, William P. Bannister, Homer E. A. Dick, Robert F. Wagner, Mark W. Potter, John B. Stanchfield, Delancey Nicoll, and William E. Slevin.

[11]McGeorge Bundy and Henry L. Stimson, *On Active Service in Peace and War* (New York: Harper, 1948), p. 72.

[12]Frederick C. Tanner to Elihu Root, April 10, 1915, Elihu Root Papers.

[13]It was Tanner who presented the resolution on the short ballot at the important December 5, 1913, party meeting. See pp. 54-55.

102　THE NEW YORK STATE CONSTITUTIONAL CONVENTION

[14]Edgar T. Brackett to Elihu Root, April 8, 1915, Elihu Root Papers.

[15]John Lord O'Brian, *The Reminiscences of John Lord O'Brian* (New York: Columbia University Oral History Research Office, 1952), pp. 147-148.

[16]Root did appoint Brackett chairman of the Committee on Legislative Organization.

[17]Barnes took part in the effort to secure the chairmanship of Judiciary for Brackett (see William Barnes to Elihu Root, April 10, 1915, Elihu Root Papers).

[18]Ray B. Smith, ed., *History of the State of New York, Political and Governmental*, 6 vols. (Syracuse, The Syracuse Press Inc., 1922), vol. 4: *History of the State of New York, Political and Governmental, 1896-1920*, by Roscoe C.E. Brown, p. 260.

[19]Gregory Mason, "Rebuilding A Constitution: Editorial Correspondence from Albany," *The Outlook* 110 (August 18, 1915):904.

[20]Frederick C. Tanner, *The Oral History of Frederick C. Tanner*, 2 vols. (New York: Columbia University Oral History Research Office, 1950) 1:139. John Lord O'Brian agreed with this assessment of Barnes' role in the Convention, see O'Brian, p. 165.

[21]Their cooperation was facilitated by the fact that the two committees shared common quarters in the state Senate finance committee room.

[22]This was the third largest number of proposed amendments to be referred to a single committee. The largest number, 153, was referred to the committee on the judiciary, and the second largest, 77, to the committee on the Bill of Rights. Following the Tanner committee came the committee on legislative powers, with 55; the committee on legislative organization, with 48; and then the Stimson committee, with 44. (These figures were provided by George A. Blauvelt, "The Work of the Constitutional Convention," *Cornell Law Quarterly* 1 [November 1915]:20.)

[23]Delaney was the first witness to appear before the Tanner committee. After the convention, Tanner explained that he had invited Delaney to speak first in order to start the committee's work off on a bipartisan basis. It was the Republican legislature which had abolished the Department of Efficiency and Economy in March—and with it, Delaney's position—and that action was, presumably, a judgment on the quality of the department's work. Tanner wanted to show that while he was a party man, he would seek advice and counsel wherever he believed he could find it. In fact, his decision to call Delaney first alienated some party members, chief among whom was Governor Charles Whitman who interpreted Tanner's action as a distinct slap at the Republican legislature and at him as he had backed the legislature's decision. Tanner told Whitman that he felt Delaney's ideas could be useful to the committee and that this was the only thing that mattered. He also added:

> "Governor, you have been elected to do one job—that of the Governor of this state. In perhaps a smaller way I have been elected by the people as a delegate to the Constitutional Convention, and Senator Root has put me as chairman of what he considers perhaps the most important Committee of this Convention. While I will be glad to receive your advice, I am going to ride my own line, and you might as well understand it now" (Tanner 1:133-134).

[24]Ibid., p. 135.

[25]Ibid., pp. 135-136. After the convention, in a 1916 visit he paid to Oyster Bay, Tanner told Roosevelt the reason for the decision not to invite him. Roosevelt concurred with the reasoning, saying "You're damn right; it would have been troublesome" (Ibid., p. 136).

[26]Henry L. Stimson to William H. Taft, May 28, 1915, Henry L. Stimson Papers. The invitation to Taft affords another example of careful planning by Stimson and Tanner. Stimson followed up the invitation with a letter to Frederick A. Cleveland asking him to draft a memo on the subject of an executive budget for Taft to study prior to testifying (Henry L. Stimson to Frederick A. Cleveland, June 1, 1915, Henry L. Stimson Papers). Stimson also sent a second letter to Taft, detailing his positions on a short ballot, consolidation of administrative agencies, and an executive budget, and asking Taft to support them in his testimony (Henry L. Stimson to William H. Taft, June 1, 1915, Henry L. Stimson Papers).

²⁷Charles A. Beard, "The New York Constitutional Convention," *National Municipal Review* 4 (October 1915):640.

²⁸This feature of the executive budget amendment may safely be attributed to Stimson's personal influence on the committee. It was a favorite of his which dated from his first public statement on state reorganization (see p. 51) and with which he had become identified—many other reorganization advocates did not mention, much less emphasize, this particular concept.

²⁹The other departments the amendment provided for were: Public Utilities, to consist of two, five-member commissions appointed by the governor with the advice and consent of the Senate; Conservation, to be directed by a nine member commission similarly appointed; Civil Service, to be directed by three commissioners similarly appointed; Education, whose chief administrative officer (no title was cited) would be appointed by the Regents of the State University; and State, Taxation and Finance, Public Works, Health, Agriculture, Charities and Corrections, Banking, Insurance, and Labor and Industry, all of whose heads would be appointed by the governor with the advice and consent of the Senate.

³⁰In the 30 year period from 1885 to 1914, state expenditures increased by nearly 600 percent, while population increased by only 82 percent, and personal property liable to taxation, by only 274 percent (New York State, Constitutional Convention, 1915, *Journal of the Constitutional Convention, 1915* [Albany: J. B. Lyon Co., Printers, 1915] p. 385).

³¹Ibid., p. 390.

³²Ibid.

³³Ibid., pp. 390-391.

³⁴Ibid., pp. 393-394.

³⁵The only potent argument cited, and worth noting, was that the amendment would reduce the power of the legislature. To this, Stimson replied by referring to his earlier arguments concerning the legislature's loss of the state's purse strings under the prevailing system, and the importance of restoring the proper relationship between the executive and the legislature (Ibid., p. 401).

Also worthy of note is that Stimson cleverly managed here, in a concluding appeal to would-be opponents of the amendment, to inject an impressive list of prominent citizens who favored an executive budget. He did this in the context of replying to the argument that since budgets were a European import, they were somehow "un-American." Stimson made several responses to this, among them that an idea advocated by such people as Presidents Taft and Wilson, and Senators George H. Pendleton, James G. Blaine, John J. Ingalls, W. B. Allison, O. H. Platt, Elihu Root, and James W. Wadsworth, could hardly be considered un-American! (Ibid., p. 402.)

³⁶Ibid., p. 457.

³⁷Ibid., p. 458.

³⁸While the report was not, as was noted, the open bid for support that the Stimson report was, it must be said that it took pains not to alienate any of its readers. It stressed that its dissatisfaction was with the state administrative system, not with the people or administrations who operated the system:

> "The changes recommended in this report are not written as a criticism of any individual either in this or in previous administrations. The criticism is one of the defective system under which our public servants have labored at great disadvantage to render public service. The machinery of government is built wrongly and no one under present conditions can make it work well" (Ibid., p. 457).

It also took note of the fact that the popular dissatisfaction with the system was bipartisan, quoting liberally from both the Republican and Democratic parties' 1914 platforms (Ibid., pp. 459-460).

³⁹How Root "guessed wrong" in appointing Baldwin to the committee is unclear. There is, of course, the possibility that he appointed Baldwin for extraneous political reasons after he had ensured a healthy proreorganization majority on the committee.

⁴⁰New York, *Journal of the Constitutional Convention, 1915*, pp. 465-466.

[41]This influence was exercised chiefly through his selections for the two committees. But it was also undoubtedly exercised through the advice and counsel he offered the committees during their work. For Root was in constant contact with all the committees, making his own feelings known on the proposals they were entertaining. A contemporary account stated:

> "During the sessions [of the committees] Mr. Root was indefatigable, going from committee to committee, pleading, arguing, and threatening. . . . By the time the first proposition was ready for its final hearing before the Committee of the Whole, Senator Root was the supreme influence in the Convention" (Mason, p. 904).

[42]Beard, p. 640.

[43]Referring to the fact that the amendment left the positions of comptroller and attorney general on the ballot, the Tanner report spoke of "the peculiar relation which these two officers hold to the people of the state as a whole" (New York, *Journal of the Constitutional Convention, 1915*, p. 461). This suggests that the basis for compromise was philosophical, i.e., that there was a positive principle arguing for leaving the positions elective, rather than an attempt to attract support for the amendment, and that the reorganization advocates would have left these positions elective even if they did not have to be concerned about attracting support. In fact, this was not the case. In discussing this compromise before the convention, Tanner made no mention whatsoever of a substantive argument for keeping the positions elective (New York, *Revised Record*, 3:3330-3331). And after the convention he wrote that had he been physically fit—he was plagued by bouts of appendicitis throughout the convention—he could have brought the ballot down to just the governor and lieutenant governor and convinced the convention to adopt a shorter ballot than it did! (Tanner, 2:154.) The report must therefore be seen as an attempt by the reorganization advocates to save face by rationalizing what they felt they had to do in order to gain broad support.

[44]One harsh critic was H. S. Gilbertson, an officer of the National and New York Short Ballot Organizations (see H. S. Gilbertson to Henry L. Stimson, August 3, 1915, Henry L. Stimson Papers). That the critics were harder on Stimson, a mere member of the committee which had produced this short ballot, than on the chairman, Tanner, was a function of the fact that Stimson was popularly perceived, and quite correctly, to be the principal leader—along with Root—of the pro-reorganization forces in the convention. Another reason they may have been particularly annoyed with Stimson is because he served on the executive committee of the New York Short Ballot Organization.

[45]Henry L. Stimson to Richard S. Childs, July 19, 1915, Henry L. Stimson Papers.
[46]Jessup, 2:292.
[47]An exception was his designation of convention committee chairmen. For each of the 30 committees, Root had appointed a Republican chairman. However, this was undoubtedly excused by the Democrats as the accepted practice on the part of the controlling party.

[48]Root's proudest boast at the conclusion of the convention was that the convention was a nonpartisan one. In his closing remarks to the convention, he told the delegates:

> ". . . this convention has risen above the plane of partisan politics. It has refused to make itself or permit itself to be made the agency of party advantage except as faithful service for the state is a benefit to party. It has refused to engage in the play of politics. No caucus and no conference has marred the impartiality of our proceeding. No resolution has bound the judgment or conscience of any member of this convention. Our conception of our duty was to leave behind strife of party, and upon the higher plane of patriotism and love of country, to join all together, whatever our parties, in doing the best we could for the prosperity of our beloved state" (New York, *Revised Record*, 4:4380).

Though his rhetoric may have been a bit inflated, there is evidence to support Root's claim of nonpartisanship for the convention. Of the 33 measures adopted by the convention, 12 were adopted unanimously. The rest were adopted by the following majorities: 12, by more than 10 to 1; 2, by more than 7 to 1; 2, by more than 4 to 1; 2, by more than 3 to 1; and 3, by more than 2 to 1.

Considering the great majority of Republicans in the convention, Root's achievement of preventing the convention from becoming a partisan affair was no mean feat, as he acknowledged to fellow delegate Mark Potter after the convention:

"One of the very gratifying things about the Convention is that Republicans and Democrats succeeded in working together for the public interest upon so great a variety of matters. . . . I doubt if many people appreciate how hard the fight was to prevent the convention, with its enormous Republican majority, from being turned into a party agency" (Elihu Root to Mark Potter, October 16, 1915, Elihu Root Papers).

[49]No such argument, on the other hand, could be made on behalf of the short ballot and the consolidation of agencies. There, the case rested exclusively on the need for responsibility in government, and that this need, in turn, necessitated the strengthening of the governor.

[50]New York, *Revised Record*, 2:1609.

[51]Ibid., p. 1613.

[52]Ibid., p. 1632-1633.

[53]Ibid., p. 1613.

[54]Ibid., p. 1607. By this, Stimson meant that there was only one dissenting vote. That was Robert F. Wagner's.

[55]It was probably primarily to this that Frederck C. Mosher referred when he wrote that: "The ideology of the executive budget has perhaps never been more forcefully expressed than by Stimson on the floor of the 1915 Convention" (Frederick C. Mosher, "The Executive Budget, Empire State Style" *Public Administration Review* 12 [Spring 1952]:78).

[56]Chief among these delegates was Al Smith, who pointed out that the effect of this compromise was that the proposed plan convered only one half of the state's expenditures:

". . . the proposal set forth by the Committee on Finance, and so well and ably explained by the gentleman from New York, to my way of thinking does not go half far enough, because as a matter of fact that proposed budgetary reform reaches only about one-half of the appropriations of the State. Now I take it that the budget, so called, will be what is known to-day as the Appropriation Bill, or the bill commonly known as the one that makes provision for the maintenance of the State government. In the year just passed that bill amounted to $32,000,000, but there were $63,000,000 appropriated by the Legislature, so that there are $31,000,000 still left to be taken care of by the system so much fault has been found with" (New York, *Revised Record*, 2:1635).

[57]The critics who believed the amendment did not go far enough made it clear that they would support it even if no changes were made.

[58]Explaining why he referred to the prevailing system as "the system from which we are about to depart," he stated: "Because I recognize the fact that the change is to be made" (New York, *Revised Record*, 2:1679).

[59]Ibid., p. 1678.

[60]Ibid., pp. 1679-1680.

[61]Ibid., p. 1683.

[62]It should be pointed out that the debate over this issue—whether the legislature's loss of the initiating function diminished its role in the budgetary process, as Brackett argued, or, that when seen in the context of the whole executive budget system, actually enhanced it, as argued Stimson—did not go beyond statements of the respective positions. At no time did Brackett and Stimson come to grips with each others positions and attempt to deal with them. Brackett merely emphasized the loss of the initiating function, and Stimson, the executive budget system as a whole.

[63]New York, *Revised Record*, 2:1770. In fact, Brackett took the floor later in the debates to speak against the executive budget again. This was on August 18, when he rose to introduce and have read to the convention a letter by State Senator Elon Brown which decried reorganization in general and the executive budget in particular. As it happened, Stimson was prepared for this and countered by introducing a letter from Columbia University President Nicholas Murray Butler which warmly endorsed the executive budget (Ibid., 3:2335-2339).

[64]These were the votes of John T. Dooling, Mat Endres, and William S. Ostrander.

[65]John Lord O'Brian judged the short ballot, the most "acutely discussed" issue in the convention (O'Brian, p. 156).

[66]New York, *Revised Record*, 4:3372. This statement of Tanner's, made before the convention, was quoted by Wickersham in the debates.

[67]Ibid., 3:3335. It will be recalled that at the time the platform was being voted on, Brackett argued against it, predicting that its "non-binding" nature would be ignored by the reorganization advocates who would urge party loyalty! (See p. 62.)

[68]There were, of course, others who spoke against the short ballot as well. One of these, Lemuel Quigg, made an interesting point which Brackett did not touch on. Quigg complained of the pressure Tanner was exerting on the delegates to support the short ballot. He did not specify the manner in which this pressure was being applied, but indicated that it had to do with Tanner's position as state chairman (Ibid., 4:3366). This confirms our assumption that Tanner—and Root, Stimson, and Wickersham—used whatever influence he (they) had with the delegates on behalf of reorganization during the debates. Unfortunately, there is no record of just how and on what specific occasions this influence was used.

[69]Ibid., p. 3418.

[70]Ibid., pp. 3421-3442.

[71]Brackett's charge was, of course, a valid one (see pp. 56-60).

[72]New York, *Revised Record*, 4:3427.

[73]Ibid., p. 3453.

[74]Ibid., pp. 3461-3462.

[75]O'Brian, p. 148.

[76]New York, *Revised Record*, 4:3494-3495.

[77]Ibid., pp. 3501-3503.

[78]Ibid., pp. 3504-3505.

[79]Indeed, when earlier in the debate Lemuel Quigg spoke against the short ballot, he predicted the nature of Root's address, should the latter decide to speak, in the following manner:

> "We all know if this amendment really gets into peril it will be expected, hoped for, desired, depended on by those in advocacy of it, that Mr. Root will take the floor. Now I tell you this. If he does, he will not lift here any 'Cross of Gold' or crown of thorns. With my knowledge of him for thirty odd years, he will address all his remarks to the heads of this Convention, the intellects of it, and not to the feet of it" (Ibid., p. 3367).

[80]O'Brian, pp. 184-185.

[81]Childs, pp. 7-8.

[82]Childs recalled that "a good anticlimax" to Root's address "was furnished by a little upstate man with a weak voice who was attempting to make a feeble answer to Elihu Root" (Ibid., p. 8). The "little man" was Charles H. Betts, and no one who followed him made a much more potent answer. As for the reorganization advocates, they rested their case with Root's address.

[83]Unlike the first, the second amendment was not adopted in exactly the same form as it had come out of committee. Originally, the amendment had provided for 15 departments (see n. 29). The convention added two departments, splitting the Department of Taxation and Finance into two departments which would handle the two functions separately, and creating a Treasury Department.

[84]New York Bureau of Municipal Research, "The Budget Idea in the United States," *Municipal Research*. no. 69 (January 1916), p. 64.

[85]While this was a major reform in New York State, it could not be considered a "first" for some other states had short ballots at this time. New York's neighbor, New Jersey, for example, voted only for a governor statewide.

[86]Charles A. Beard, "The Budgetary Provisions of the New York Constitution," *The Annals of the American Academy of Political and Social Science* 62 (November 1915):68.

[87]New York, *Revised Record*, 4:3374.

[88]This attitude towards the convention's decision on the manner of submission, and whether or not it was justified, will be closely examined in Chapter 4.

Chapter 4

The Voters Decide

The reorganization advocates recognized that the campaign for ratification would not be an easy one. To begin with, there would be several groups of oppositionists. Brackett and his allies in the convention did not, of course, speak only for themselves, but as representatives of a substantial number of people in the northern regions of the state who shared their views on reorganization. These people would be unyielding in their opposition to the new constitution. Then, on a more limited scale, there would be opposition at the other extreme. The small but vocal group of thorough going reformers for whom compromise, however small, meant capitulation, had been severely critical of the relatively minor compromises agreed to by the reorganization advocates in the convention. They had rejected the arguments made by Stimson and others that it was unrealistic to expect to accomplish at once all that they wanted, and that it was foolish not to accept all that they could get for the present. Now, at the close of the convention, they remained unmoved by these arguments and were resolved to defeat the constitution.[1] A third group of oppositionists would be the small group of Root's political rivals in the Republican party who cared little one way or another about reorganization, but who understood that an affirmative vote on the document would be considered a personal triumph for the chief driving force behind it, Root, and that this success would help him immeasurably if he decided to seek his party's nomination for President in 1916.[2] They were determined to deny him this nomination and, therefore, to defeat the constitution. This last group was especially feared by the reorganization advocates,[3] and with good reason, as we shall see.

Of far greater concern to the reorganization advocates than these groups of oppositionists who, even collectively, did not constitute a very large portion of the electorate were the masses of voters throughout the state who were uneducated on the need for reorganization and who could not be expected to vote for fundamental changes without achieving some understanding of this need. The task of educating these voters in the brief six-week period between the convention's adjournment and election day was a formidable one. It was made even more difficult by the fact that the issue of the new constitution would be competing for public attention with an on-going event on which public attention had been riveted for months, the European war. Years later, Stimson described the focus of public attention in this period in this way:

> The summer of 1915 was one of increasing tension, as America watched the great battle in Europe, and President Wilson carried on his intricate maneuvers with the Germans. The *Lusitania* had been sunk in May, and after that the war, and its possible effect on America, far outshadowed the problems of state government which had been pushed forward by a small group of men in the face of public apathy.[4]

Combined with the factor of limited time, this competition for attention ensured that the effort to educate the electorate on reorganization would be quite a struggle.

Recognizing these obstacles even as they did, the reorganization advocates were, nevertheless, confident of ultimate victory.[5] To some extent, this confidence was based on the success with which previous constitutional conventions had met in New York State. That the voters had in the past ratified three of the four constitutions framed by constitutional conventions[6] was indicative of the faith the people traditionally had in the work of their constitutional conventions. It was safe to assume that some of this traditional trust would extend to the work of this constitutional convention. More than the encouraging history of constitutional conventions in New York State, however, what inspired the confidence of the reorganization advocates was their belief that the constitution they had produced, with its revolutionary reorganization amendments, was an excellent one—if they did not all believe with delegate Louis Marshall that it was "the best Constitution that has ever been presented to the people of any state in the Union,"[7] their evaluations were only slightly more modest—and that this excellence would not fail to be noticed by the people. Admittedly, it would not be easy to combat the influence of the oppositionist groups and to overcome the limits of time and the competition for public attention, but they had the advantage of representing a work which was the answer to many of the state's problems, and while they would encounter difficulties in attempting to make their case, once they had been heard, their work would surely commend itself to the voters.

To help make their case, the reorganization advocates formed, in the closing days of the convention, a Committee for the Adoption of the Constitution. The committee would print and disseminate literature on the constitution and coordinate the speaking activities of the leading reorganization advocates throughout the campaign. Centrally headquartered in Albany, the committee's chairman was Senator James W. Wadsworth, chosen because he was an upstate Republican who wielded considerable influence among his neighbors;[8] and its vice chairman was Alton B. Parker, a prominent Democrat who would presumably help give the committee a bipartisan image. Much was expected from this committee and its existence was a source of optimism to the reorganization advocates. Stimson, for example, contrasted the situation in 1915 with that in 1894 when there was no concerted effort to campaign for ratification of the new constitution. The fact that the 1894 constitution was overwhelmingly approved despite the absence of such an effort made him "feel pretty confident" that the 1915 constitution would be ratified.[9]

THE CAMPAIGN FOR RATIFICATION

From the start, the campaign held a series of jolts for the reorganization advocates. The opposition they had expected materialized, but along with it there appeared opposition of a different nature which, because of the great numbers of people involved, was far more serious. This opposition consisted of groups of people who were not necessarily opposed to the reorganization amendments in themselves, but who opposed the constitution as a whole because of other items in it which they considered objectionable, or because it did not contain items they felt should have been included. The reorganization advocates did not expect this. As we have seen, they reasoned that as reorganization was the most controversial subject in the convention, it would be on the reorganization amendments that the campaign for ratification would focus, with little or no attention paid the other amendments. As to items the constitution left out which some would have liked to have seen included, they were either unaware of these or underestimated the degree of interest in them. For these reasons, they consented to have the reorganization amendments presented to the electorate together with the other amendments and to campaign for the constitution as a whole. This was a grievous error (more will be said about this error later) as they found out in the opening days of the campaign.

One of the first groups to come out against the constitution was organized labor. The executive council of the State Federation of Labor had met in Albany on May 24 and 25 to formulate amendments on labor related matters which it would present to the constitutional convention. At the conclusion of the meetings it sent to all the delegates 24 "suggestions" and eight amendments.[10] Among other things, the proposals would have provided for: a guarantee of continuous administration of labor affairs by making the labor commissioner a constitutional officer; a state fund for workmen's compensation; the power to protect the health and welfare of women and children in industry; old age pensions; a trade disputes law; and a guarantee that military tribunals would under no circumstances exercise jurisdiction over citizens while the regularly constituted state courts were open to administer justice, an important point to labor because of their fear that such tribunals would be used against striking workers, and because the legality of this use of tribunals under the prevailing laws was unclear and a subject of some debate.

Labor was not optimistic about the treatment their proposals would receive from the convention. They did not enjoy substantial representation in the convention[11] and many of the delegates were unsympathetic to labor. They were, therefore, not surprised when the great majority of their proposals was rejected. But the fact that it was expected did not lessen their disappointment over their defeat. They were especially bitter over the relatively close defeat—by a vote of 65 to 50—of the proposal to rule out the possibility of using military tribunals to prosecute citizens while the regular courts were open. They believed this to be a real threat against striking workers because of the recent experience in West Virginia where such tribunals had been used against strikers. Moreover, they believed that the convention, by debating the proposal and rejecting it, had made matters worse than they previously were, as former Court of Appeals Chief Justice Cullen, an ally of labor on this issue, explained:

The failure of the constitution to forbid the trial of civilians by military tribunals after the debate on the subject will be argued in every court where the question arises as proving that the people did not intend to prevent the judiciary from authorizing such trials should it see fit, and that the guarantee of jury trial must be considered subordinate to such power.[12]

The defeat of the proposal on military tribunals along with the defeat of most of their other proposals assured labor's opposition to the constitution.[13] By a unanimous vote of state labor leaders meeting in Albany on October 4, it was decided to oppose and actively campaign against the constitution. Handbills describing labor's dissatisfaction with the constitution were drawn up and distributed throughout the state and committees were organized to attend local union meetings and urge the members to vote against the constitution. In an unprecedented display of unity,[14] all segments of organized labor in the state cooperated to try and defeat the constitution.

Another group to come out against the constitution consisted of municipal employees such as firemen, policemen, and teachers. The portion of the constitution that had earned it their enmity was its home rule provision which, in a departure from past practice, authorized each city in the state to regulate the compensation and method of removal of its employees. Previously, these had come under the jurisdiction of the state legislature, an arrangement which was popular with municipal employees for two reasons. First, employees of one city could count on the support of similar employees in other cities in bringing pressure to bear on the legislature to act favorably toward them. Thus, Buffalo firemen negotiating a salary increase would be supported before the legislature by their brethren throughout the state. Second, by having the question of their compensation decided in a place far removed from their home communities, they could risk making unreasonable demands with the assurance that such demands would be less visible to the home town voters than if they would have had to negotiate with their local governments. The new constitution would eliminate these negotiating advantages and, accordingly, municipal employees across the state opposed it.

A third group to oppose the constitution took exception to its provision for safeguarding the natural resources of the state. This provision created a Department of Conservation, to be headed by nine commissioners, whose function it would be to encourage forestry, maintain the state's forest preserve, prevent the pollution of its waters, and protect its fish, birds and game. These functions had, in the past, been in the hands of several separate, and often overlapping, boards and commissions,[15] and their consolidation into one central agency would clearly be an improvement. Nevertheless, some conservationists objected to such an agency on the grounds that its governing board, the nine commissioners, would be dominated by the lumber and water power interests which would place a higher value on their profits than on conservation. Just why they thought these interests would necessarily dominate the Conservation Department's governing board they never made clear.

The closest they came to making an argument was in an open letter to conservationists by George A. Sawyer, president of the New York State Fish, Game and Forest League, in which he asserted that the fact that the author of the conservation amendment, Ferris J. Meigs, was also president of the Santa Clara Lumber Company, was an indication that the new agency would probably serve the lumber and water power interests.[16] This argument was not, of course, a very logical one, but it was enough to create some suspicion in the minds of many conservationists in the state, a good number of whom decided that it would be safer to retain the prevailing system and to vote against the constitution.

One other major group in the state came out against the constitution and, while its position may have come as a surprise to some because of its largely positive attitude during the convention's work, this position was, in fact, entirely consistent with its long-standing aims. This group consisted of Tammany Hall Democrats who had generally been, as we have seen, cooperative in the convention, but who now chose to oppose its final product. Their opposition is not difficult to explain. Their sole motivation in seeking a constitutional convention had been to gain an opportunity to rewrite the constitution's reapportionment provision which, they felt, discriminated against preponderately Democratic New York City. Having failed to do so in this constitutional convention because of the huge Republican majority, they now looked forward to 1916 when, by provision of the prevailing constitution, the people would once again vote on whether or not to hold a constitutional convention. The likelihood that the electorate would approve another convention so soon after this one was small in any event, but it would be even less likely if this convention was successful. The only way that there would be a reasonable chance of convincing the people to hold another convention was to defeat the proposed constitution. It was with this in mind that Tammany urged its followers to vote against the constitution.[17]

In addition to these unexpected groups of oppositionists, the reorganization advocates had to contend with the opposition they expected. And here, too, the campaign held some surprises, albeit milder. One surprise was the intensity of the opposition of the anti-reorganization upstate Republicans. In the convention debates, their chief spokesman, Brackett, had always tempered his criticisms of reorganization with the admission that he could not honestly claim that the implementation of any or all of the reorganization measures would by itself create an autocracy. The only claim he made was that these measures were undemocratic by nature and would help create a climate for the introduction of further undemocratic measures, all of which would ultimately result in an autocracy. In the campaign, however, the upstate Republicans were not as careful in their denunciations of reorganization and the new constitution. Entirely representative of the tenor of their campaign against the constitution was the attack by delegate Lemuel Quigg, who together with Brackett and State Sentator Elon Brown led the upstate opposition:

> Taking, then, these new provisions as to the Governor's power of appointment and removal, the consolidation of all the activities of government into his hands and the grant to him of full power over the public purse, I am obliged to report to you that in my view this is an attempt to create in New York a novel government, the like of which does not today exist on earth; that it provides an absolute despotism, with permission to you to change the despot once in two years, if, with his complete control over the government, he does not succeed in proving stronger than you are.[18]

The upstate Republican opposition framed the question of whether to vote for or against the constitution as a choice between democracy or an immediate autocracy. And, faced with such a choice, they loudly proclaimed, the voters could not but reject the constitution.

Another surprise was the extent of opposition to the constitution based on what a successful outcome would mean for Root's personal political fortunes. Initially, the reorganization advocates had expected such opposition to be limited to Root's few Republican rivals. Instead, they found that it extended to a group from whom they had actually expected support, the Progressives. Assuming that the Progressives would find much to their liking in the reorganization amendments, Root had written to Progressive leader George W. Perkins on September 9 inviting him to join a citizens committee which would work for ratification of the constitution. Not only did Perkins decline Root's invitation, he made it known that he was opposed to the constitution and would work for its defeat.

Perkins gave several reasons for his opposition, among them, that the short ballot was not short enough, that the proposed Conservation Department would be dominated by the lumber and water power interests, and that the proposed consolidation of agencies would result in abolition of the Department of Markets, a favorite of Perkins'. There is no reason to question his sincerity in these objections to the constitution, but it is also true that he left a principal reason for his opposition unstated. This was his, and the Progressives', animosity toward Root which, to the surprise and disappointment of the reorganization advocates, outweighed whatever they might have found appealing in the constitution. This animosity dated from the 1912 Republican national convention when Root, as chairman of the convention, presided over the defeat of the pro-Roosevelt forces. The Progressives were aware that popular approval of the constitution would be considered a personal victory for Root and that it would greatly enhance his changes for the 1916 Republican Presidential nomination. It was in large part, for this reason that they opposed the constitution and worked actively against ratification.[19]

The reorganization advocates struggled valiantly against all this opposition. Wherever they could, they rebutted the substantive arguments made against the constitution. Where they could not, they used other means to counterbalance the influence of the oppositionists.

In a publication of the Committee for the Adoption of the Constitution[20] drawn up specifically to address the issue, Root answered labor's primary objection to the constitution, the absence of a provision prohibiting the use of military tribunals against civilians. Root argued that the constitution already contained what was tantamount to such a prohibition in its declaration that "the trial by jury in all cases in which it has been heretofore used shall remain inviolate forever."[21] To the probable rejoinder that this provision was an insufficient safeguard, as it did not rule out tribunals explicitly, Root wrote that, in fact, no additional safeguard would necessarily prevent the use of tribunals. For the West Virginia case in which tribunals had been used against striking workers, and because of which the New York labor movement had become so sensitive to the issue, had actually occurred despite an explicit prohibition in the West Virginia constitution against the use of tribunals.[22] The West Virginia courts had upheld the action on a legal technicality—they ruled that the strike had represented an "insurrection" in which case the constitution itself could be suspended—and similar technicalities could probably be found to get around any prohibition New York could devise. Labor was thus as safe as they could be with the current constitutional provision, concluded Root.

In an effort to regain the support of some of the disaffected municipal employees, the committee released the text of a letter by Root to John H. Finley of the State Education Department, in which the former advised the latter that education would remain under the jurisdiction of the state and that municipal employees working in the area of education would continue to deal directly with the legislature regarding their compensation and method of removal.[23] In addition, it reprinted a letter written by delegate Meir Steinbrink to the *Civil Service Chronicle* which assured all municipal employees that at least in regard to methods of removal, they would still retain the right to appeal individual instances of dismissal to the legislature.[24]

To the conservationists in the state, the committee wrote of the constitution's conservation provision that "no other article of the proposed Constitution has been subjected to so much ignorant and malicious representation."[25] It pointed out that the provision's sole objective was to replace the chaotic structure which had traditionally been charged with conservation matters, and that, far from delivering the state's natural resources into the hands of the anti-conservationist interests, it would put the state into a better position to conserve them. The committee also made use of an open letter to conservationists written by J. S. Whipple, a Salamanca, New York, attorney. Whipple argued that George A. Sawyer, who led the conservationist opposition and who purported to speak for the organization he headed, the New York State Fish, Game and Forest League, could not fairly claim to represent that organization in his opposition. Whipple pointed out that Sawyer had initially called a meeting of the executive committee of the League and asked them to oppose the constitution on conservationist principles. When he was voted down, he proceeded to call, on just five days notice, a general meeting of the league membership. Only 16 of the state's 74 member clubs were able to send representatives to the meeting and it was representatives of this small number of clubs that voted on a resolution against the constitution. The resolution carried by a vote of 20 to 12. When seen in the light of these facts, concluded Whipple, Sawyer's contention that the league was opposed to the constitution became far less impressive.[26]

To Democratic voters, the committee pointed out the support for the constitution voiced by such prominent Democrats as Alton B.

Parker, Morgan J. O'Brien, Delancey Nicoll, D. Cady Herrick, and Francis L. Stetson, among others.[27] The reorganization advocates hoped that this list of supporters would influence some Democrats, but they were under no illusion that it could counterbalance the influence of Tammany Hall, "the most powerful, efficient, corrupt political machine in the history of urban America."[28] Indeed, their response to the Tammany opposition was not so much to fight it among Democrats as to use it as leverage among Republicans. That is, they pointed out to Republicans,[29] and especially to the upstate oppositionists, that it was Tammany Hall's objective to defeat the constitution in order to increase the likelihood of a new convention in 1916 in which it would gain a fresh opportunity to secure the reapportionment it had long sought. As there was no guarantee that Republicans would control a 1916 convention, the possibility of this reapportionment was a real one and if only for this reason alone, Republicans would do well to vote for the constitution despite its shortcomings! In this way, the reorganization advocates turned some of the opposition into an advantage in appealing for support from others.

Beyond responding to individual groups of oppositionists, the reorganization advocates conducted, through the committee, a massive campaign aimed at educating the large number of people who had not formed an opinion on the new constitution, on the merits of reorganization and the constitution. They believed that these people represented the majority of voters in the state and that even if all of the committee's efforts to change the minds of the oppositionists failed, they could still be successful if they won over the as yet uncommitted. The principal features of their campaign were large-scale distributions of pro-constitution literature—a total of two million pieces of literature were distributed according to one report[30]—and personal appearances throughout the state by the leading proponents of the constitution, including Root, Stimson, Tanner, and Seth Low. The campaign relied especially heavily on the appearances by these men who gave unstintingly of their time and energy. Stimson, like others, spent most of the time between early September and election day stumping for the constitution, to the neglect of his legal practice and personal affairs, and Tanner later recalled that in a not unrepresentative itinerary for these men, he ". . . went all the way from Riverhead and Patchogue, Long Island to Buffalo, and spoke before Rotary Clubs, Chambers of Commerce, in synagogues, in churches, before Merchants Associations, and social clubs."[31]

Despite their dismay at the nature and extent of the opposition, the reorganization advocates remained confident that the constitution would be ratified. They believed that at least some of their rebuttals to the individual groups of oppositionists would be effective and that their campaign of popular education would attract the support of the undecided. To be sure, their optimism was not based on any real information as to the attitude of the electorate. Rather, it was merely an intuitive feeling based on the aforementioned faith they had in the quality of their work. But they were no less convinced of their ultimate success than if they would have had real evidence of widespread support. Thus, Stimson wrote, on October 28, that he thought "the chances of the constitution are rapidly improving with every day. I think it will carry, and very likely by a much larger vote than we expect."[32] And Tanner predicted, on October 29, that the constitution would carry by a "fifty thousand majority."[33]

It was for this reason that the outcome of the vote on November 2 came as a surprise to the reorganizaton advocates. The constitution was defeated 910,462 to 400,423, a vote of more than two to one. The reorganization advocates were genuinely puzzled, not to say disappointed. "It is a curious situation that nobody . . . realized at all what the tremendous verdict against [the constitution] was going to be,"[34] wrote Stimson, one day after the vote. In truth, however, the defeat of the constitution, and the wide margin of defeat, should not have been unexpected. For there were several reasons behind the defeat, most of them already touched on in the course of the preceding discussion, which made it entirely understandable and which were visible all along to the disinterested observer, if not to those emotionally involved in the contest. Indeed, upon reflection in the days following the vote, the reorganization advocates themselves conceded this.

REASONS FOR THE DEFEAT OF THE CONSTITUTION

First and foremost of the reasons behind the defeat of the constitution was the manner of its submission to the voters. The fact that it was submitted as a whole for the voters to approve or reject in toto, rather than in separate amendments or small groups of amendments, assured the constitution of many more enemies than it would otherwise have had. Individuals, or groups, who were opposed to only one item in the constitution had no chioce but to vote against the entire constitution. On the other hand, people who would have liked to have seen certain items in the constitution which were left out, were far more likely to register their protests by voting against the document as a whole than by voting against a series of separately offered amendments, some of which may well have appealed to them. The decision to submit the constitution as a whole substantially reduced the chances for ratification from the outset.

This seems so logical that it is difficult to understand why it went completely unrecognized by the reorganization advocates at the time of the decision on the manner of submission.[35] For it did go unrecognized. Herbert Parsons, a leading reorganization advocate in the convention, had been chairman of the committee on the time and manner of submission of the revised constitution, and he, along with a majority of his committee, recommended to the convention that it submit the constitution as a whole. In the ensuing debate no reorganization advocate of any stature raised his voice to question the wisdom of submission as a whole and the single one who participated in the debate, Stimson, spoke in favor of this manner of submission.[36] What makes this non-recognition of the dangers of submission as a whole even more difficult to understand is that they were explicitly warned in the convention debates of these dangers. Delegate Russel Wiggins issued a general warning:

> . . . if every one of these particular articles on which objection is made gets 50,000 votes, it means 50,000 votes against all the articles together and these votes, coming from different persons and coming from the different sections opposed to them, would mean enough negative votes to destroy much that the people would otherwise be in favor of.[37]

And delegate Harry W. Neuburger offered a specific example of how submission as a whole would hurt the constitution's chances by referring to the opposition of municipal employees to the constitution's home rule provision:

> I hold no brief for any class of employees in the city of New York, but it does seem to me that the chances of success for this Constitution are being seriously impaired by submitting the home rule article as a part of the entire Constitution, for this reason: There are approximately 7,500 firemen in the city of New York; there are approximately 11,000 policemen in the city of New York. Before this Constitution is considered, before it is even submitted to the people it has something like 75,000 or 80,000 enemies. It seems inconceivable to me that men of the knowledge, information and judgment of the members of this Committee should be willing to take the chance of having 75,000 or 80,000 men, employees of the city of New York, opposed to it before it is even submitted. . . .[38]

There is, in fact, no satisfactory explanation for the position of the reorganization advocates on the question of the manner of submission.[39] At best, what can be said is that, as has been suggested earlier, the combination of their own narrow focus on reorganization and the fact that reorganization was the most controversial subject in the convention, led them to underestimate the degree of popular interest in other issues and to conclude that the campaign for ratification would revolve around the issue of reorganization. Assuming that this would be the case, they believed that it mattered not at all whether the reorganization amendments were submitted separately or as part of the larger document. As it turned out, of course, they could not have been more wrong. And they were among the first to admit it. Writing after the campaign of the decision of the reorganization advocates to go along with submission as a whole, John Lord O'Brian stated that "that method of submission was one of the most serious errors ever made by a group of intelligent men."[40] O'Brian believed that the manner of submission was one of the chief factors in the defeat of the constitution,[41] and numerous other reorganization advocates, among them Stimson[42] and Jacob Gould Schurman,[43] agreed.[44]

A second major reason behind the defeat of the constitution was the limited time available for the campaign for ratification. The convention had not been called because of a popular demand for reorganization, but for reasons completely unrelated to reorganization. Similarly, the document that the convention produced, providing for a comprehensive reorganization of the state government, was not a response to broad outside pressure for such reform, but the result of the efforts of a small group of progressive and powerful Republican reorganization advocates in the convention. Thus it was that with the close of the convention the reorganization advocates were faced with the task of educating a largely uninterested and uninformed electorate on the need for reorganization. And given the complexities of the reorganization question, to say nothing of the aforementioned competition for public attention provided by the European war, six weeks was simply too short a time in which to accomplish this. This was Stimson's conclusion in his analysis of the reasons for the defeat of the constitution:

> . . . when they returned from Albany, the sponsors of responsible government learned that in persuading the convention they had done little to persuade the voters.
>
> The central difficulty was that Stimson and his friends lacked a mandate. [The Convention's] positive reforms were not the result of the kind of prolonged public pressure which is generally required for constitutional change. Nor was there time . . . between the end of the convention and the state referendum, for the kind of educational

campaign which was the only alternative method of obtaining popular support.[45]

Root agreed with this. In a post-convention letter to Fred W. Hammond, he wrote:

> Of course, I was very sorry that the people rejected the constitution, but I suppose we should not be surprised that in a few weeks they couldn't go through the process of instruction and consideration which took the Convention between five and six months.[46]

A third principal reason behind the defeat was the political opposition to Root. As we have seen, this opposition was more extensive than was originally thought by the reorganization advocates. Charles A. Beard even suggested that at least some of the Republican opposition to reorganization on the ostensible grounds that it was undemocratic, was in reality a camouflage for the real reason for this opposition; a desire not to see Root profit politically from the success of the constitution.[47] Little could be done by the reorganization advocates against this opposition. Certainly they could not, by the time of the ratification campaign, reduce Root's personal identification with the constitution and its plan for reorganization. By then, he was considered, and rightly so, one of its chief architects and champions. Nor could they have taken steps earlier to prevent this identification. For reorganization would never have gotten as far as it did, that is, approved by the convention, were it not for the fact that it carried Root's avid sponsorship! The situation was thus not without some irony. The same sponsorship which was essential to reorganization's initial success became, in the campaign for ratification, a liability. But, ironic or not, this liability was a serious one, and it accounted, in part, for reorganization's ultimate defeat.

A fourth important reason for the defeat was the fact that the reorganization advocates did not provide, in their reorganization, for some extra form of control over the powerful executive they had created. While such a control—one popular proposal was to give the legislature the right, under certain circumstances, to call a new gubernatorial election[48]—was deemed unnecessary by the reorganization advocates, it would certainly have made their reorganization scheme more palatable to those voters who were concerned over the constitution's extensive grants of power to the executive. There is no evidence that the reorganization advocates ever seriously considered including such a feature, and at least one scholar, Margaret C. Alexander, believed that this failure to do so was the main reason behind the defeat of the constitution:

. . . the dominant factor [in the defeat of the constitution] was the
failure to provide a means of adequate control over the governor. . . .
It could not be expected that a public which had jealously confined
the executive power would suddenly enlarge the scope of that power
without imposing a prompt and effective check upon the exercise of
it.[49]

These were the principal reasons for the defeat of the constitution. There were, however, several secondary reasons as well, and
while these would not have been sufficient to doom the constitution by themselves, they were definitely negative factors and no
examination of its defeat would be complete without some mention
of them. One was the fact that the reorganization advocates did not
have at their disposal the help of someone with the capacity to
appeal to the voters on an emotional, in addition to an intellectual,
level. Writing of the defeat of the constitution, Robert S. Binkerd,
secretary of the Committee for the Adoption of the Constitution,
observed that "constitutional issues are not a matter of great
interest to Tom, Dick, and Harry, unless they are emotionally
aroused in some way," and that this was simply not done in the
campaign for ratification.[50] Root, Stimson, and the other leading
reorganization advocates were, for all their abundant talent and
intelligence, sober, dry, and distinctly unemotional figures. They
were capable of making well-reasoned arguments on behalf of their
positions, but in no way could they excite people. Stimson conceded this shortcoming and its effect on the campaign:

> Faced with the problem of securing popular support for a general
> program based on unfamiliar concepts of government, they needed a
> great teacher—a man who knew how to catch the imagination of the
> general public and enlist its backing for a cause. Stimson and others
> earnestly made speeches and wrote letters, but they lacked the
> ability to set fire to public feeling. . . .[51]

It is difficult to assess just how badly this incapacity to stir the
voters emotionally hurt the constitution's chances for ratification,
but it clearly was a factor.

Another factor was the perception of the voters of the extent to
which the convention had changed the old constitution. In addition
to making substantive changes, the convention had made numerous
stylistic ones throughout the text of the constitution in an effort to
make it more readable. These stylistic changes merely rephrased or
rearranged certain provisions and did not affect their meaning. But
they were not perceived that way by many of the voters. For, when
the revised constitution was printed for distribution to the public,
those portions of the constitution which were left unchanged were

printed in one kind of print, while the changed portions, both substantive and stylistic, were printed in another, darker kind of print. To those uninformed voters who merely glanced at the new constitution without bothering to note the difference between the substantive and the stylistic changes, it seemed as if much, if not most, of the old constitution was being changed. Naturally, this caused them to be wary of approving the constitution, which, to them, seemed like an entirely new document.

The reorganization advocates tried to correct this mistaken perception of the new constitution. In a publication of the Committee for the Adoption of the Constitution[52] they pointed out that of the constitution's 154 sections, fully 74 remained completely unchanged, while only 13 were repealed. Of the remaining 67, they continued, many were changed only slightly, with their essential meaning untouched. With many of the voters, however, it was their first impression which counted, and this impression was that virtually the entire constitution was to be replaced. These voters were undoubtedly inclined to vote against the new constitution, as Walter T. Arndt, executive secretary of the New York State Municipal Government Association and an observer of the ratification campaign, wrote:

> Unimportant and superficial as this factor [the manner in which the old and new portions of the constitution were printed] may seem, it nevertheless contributed to the result by giving the voter who attempted to study the new constitution by himself the idea that very little of the old constitution remained and that in voting for the new he was voting for a complete change in the state's basic law. This frightened many voters away.[53]

Finally, there was the fact that the period itself was not an auspicious time for constitution making in any state. For some reason, probably having to do with the public's apprehension and uncertainty over the European war and its implications for America, people were reluctant to make fundamental changes in their laws. In 1914, Wisconsin voters were asked to vote on 10 proposed amendments to the constitution and each one was voted down by large majorities. In 1915, nine proposed constitutional amendments were submitted to California voters and every one was defeated, most by overwhelming majorities. By and large, this was the case in most other states where voters were asked to pass on amendments. The situation in New York was thus not inconsistent with the experience of other states in this period. This was recognized by one contemporary scholar, Charles Crennan, who observed that:

. . . 1915 was not a propitious year for any sort of constitutional amendment. Whatever the cause—nearness of the presidential contest, the unsettled economic and political conditions due to the war—the fact is that people were in no frame of mind to adopt new proposals. More than three-fourths of the constitutional amendments voted on in the different States during the year were flatly rejected; the unwillingness of the New York electorate to change the status quo was not unique.[54]

VIEW OF THE REORGANIZATION ADVOCATES: A TEMPORARY DEFEAT

Whether their appreciation of the reasons behind the defeat of the constitution eased the disappointment of the reorganization advocates over the outcome of the vote is unclear. Indeed, considering their high hopes and their heavy investments of time and effort, it is highly unlikely that it did. What is clear, though, is that they looked upon the decision of the voters as anything but final. In words which were representative of the sentiments of most of the reorganization advocates, Stimson wrote shortly after the vote that:

> . . . [the defeat of the constitution] simply points out that we have still a long hard battle to fight before the reform of responsible government can come. But I have no greater doubt than before of its ultimate achievement.[55]

The constitution's defeat was, in the view of the reorganization advocates, but a temporary one. Their confidence in reorganization's ultimate acceptance was unshaken. And, as history has shown, their confidence was well placed.

NOTES

[1]Stimson complained bitterly in the early days of the campaign of this opposition by the more radical reorganizers, to Professors Henry J. Ford (Henry L. Stimson to Henry J. Ford, October 5, 1915, Henry L. Stimson Papers, Yale University, New Haven, CT) and Felix Frankfurter (Henry L. Stimson to Felix Frankfurter, October 11, 1915, Henry L. Stimson Papers). In his letter to the latter, he made an excellent point which was either overlooked or ignored by the radicals:

"The provoking thing . . . is that some of our unthinking reform friends seem to think that they can reject our Constitution and begin again . . . where we left off and make something better. The idiots don't seem to understand that if responsible government in the shape of this Constitution is rejected, it will be taken to be an adverse vote of the people at the polls on that cardinal subject and we won't get it again in any new Constitution."

[2]Writing of the campaign for ratification, Richard W. Leopold stated that: ". . . knowing politicians whispered that a successful outcome would stamp Root as the logical Republican candidate for the presidency in 1916" (Richard W. Leopold, *Elihu Root and the Conservative Tradition* [Boston: Little, Brown and Co., 1954], p. 94).

[3]See Henry L. Stimson to Colonel Oliver H. Payne, September 8, 1915, Henry L. Stimson Papers.

[4]McGeorge Bundy and Henry L. Stimson, *On Active Service in Peace and War* (New York: Harper, 1948), p. 78.

[5]See Henry L. Stimson to Samuel H. Beach, October 8, 1915, Henry L. Stimson Papers; James W. Wasdsworth to Frederick C. Tanner, October 1, 1915, Frederick C. Tanner Papers, Columbia University, New York, N.Y.; Jacob Gould Schurman to William Barnes, October 19, 1915, Jacob Gould Schurman Papers, Cornell University, Ithaca, N.Y.; and Samuel M. Lindsay, Secretary of the New York Bureau of Municipal Research, to Seth Low, September 18, 1915, Seth Low Papers, Columbia University, New York, N.Y.

[6]Six constitutional conventions had been held in New York State up to 1915. The first, held in 1777, did not require ratification by the electorate of the constitution it framed. The second, in 1801, was called merely to clarify some items in the 1777 constitution, not to frame a new constitution. The next four, held in 1821, 1846, 1867 and 1894 respectively, framed new constitutions which were, with the exception of the 1867 constitution, all ratified.

[7]Louis Marshall to Herbert Parsons, January 11, 1916, found in *Louis Marshall, Champion of Liberty: Selected Papers and Addresses*, ed. Charles Reznikoff, 2 vols. (Philadelphia: The Jewish Publication Society of America, 1957) 2:1008.

[8]Robert S. Binkerd, Secretary of the Committee for the Adoption of the Constitution, to Henry L. Stimson, September 23, 1915, Henry L. Stimson Papers.

[9]Henry L. Stimson to Thomas A. Kirby, October 8, 1915, Henry L. Stimson Papers.

[10]Just what the difference was between the suggestions and the amendments is not clear. Many of the suggestions would also have necessitated amending the constitution.

[11]See p. 78.

[12]Quoted in G. G. Benjamin, "The Attempted Revision of the State Constitution of New York," *American Political Science Review* 10 (February 1916):35.

[13]It should be noted that the opposition of labor's chief spokesman, Samuel Gompers, was based on more than just the convention's rejection of the labor proposals. For one thing, Gompers shared the view of the upstate Republican opposition that reorganization was undemocratic. Responding to the argument that economies could not be realized in the state government unless reorganization measures were introduced, Gompers wrote to Seth Low that "even if wasteful expenditures could not be remedied, they are much to be preferred to any remedy that surrenders freedom and the fullest exercise of control of public officials" (Samuel Gompers to Seth Low, June 25, 1915, Seth Low Papers). In addition, Henry L. Stimson believed that Gompers' opposition was in large part attributable to the fact that he was miffed because he had run as a delegate at large to the convention and lost: ". . . for Mr. Gompers the really fatal flaw [in the constitution] was in his failure of election as a delegate" (McGeorge Bundy and Henry L. Stimson, p. 77).

[14]Irwin Yellowitz, *Labor and the Progressive Movement in New York State, 1897-1916* (Ithaca: Cornell University Press, 1965), p. 241.

[15]See p. 32.

[16]Open letter by George A. Sawyer to Conservationists; copy in Frederick C. Tanner Papers.

[17]What is difficult to explain is why they were as cooperative as they were during the work of the convention if they knew they would oppose it in the end. For while Root's bipartisan attitude in the convention encouraged such cooperation (see p. 87), would it not appear contradictory to the people they would later advise to vote against the constitution? In fact, Tammany Hall did become concerned about this towards the end of the Convention when it advised its representatives to tone down their support of the Republican-backed amendments. Frederick C. Tanner recalled after the Convention that on August 27, Al Smith approached him and, referring to the ongoing debate on the short ballot, said, "Fred, I've got to pull out on you in this debate." When Tanner asked him why, Smith replied, "Well, I had a telephone call

from the old man last night," meaning Tammany boss Charles Murphy (Frederick C. Tanner, *The Oral History of Frederick C. Tanner* 2 vols. [New York: Columbia University Oral History Research Office, 1950] 2:158). True to his word, Smith became, from that point on, far less outspoken in favor of the short ballot. Why Tammany did not act sooner to discourage Democratic cooperation is unclear.

[18]Lemuel Quigg, *Mr. Quigg to His Constituents: Concerning the Constitutional Convention and Its Work*, p. 6; copy in Frederick C. Tanner Papers.

[19]This is the conclusion of Perkins' biographer, John A. Garraty (John A. Garraty, *Right-Hand Man: The Life of George W. Perkins* [New York: Harper and Brothers, Publishers, 1957] pp. 320-326). See especially pp. 325-326.

[20]Committee for the Adoption of the Constitution, *Rights of Citizens Not in Danger*, Committee Publication no. 9 (Albany, 1915).

[21]New York, *Constitution* (1894), art. 1, sec. 2, Francis N. Thorpe, ed., *The Federal and State Constitutions* 7 vols. (Washington: Government Printing Office, 1909) 5:2694.

[22]"The military shall be subordinate to the civil power and no citizen unless engaged in the military service of the state, shall be tried or punished by any military court for any offense that is cognizable by the civil courts of the state" (W. Virginia *Constitution* [1872], art. 3, sec. 12, ibid., 7:4036).

[23]Committee for the Adoption of the Constitution, *To Friends of Education*, Committee Publication no. 11 (Albany, 1915).

[24]Idem, *Right of Court Review Not Abolished*, Committee Publication no. 13 (Albany, 1915).

[25]Idem, *The Truth About the Conservation Article*, Committee Publication no. 17 (Albany, 1915), p. 1.

[26]Open letter by J. S. Whipple; copy in Frederick C. Tanner Papers.

[27]Committee for the Adoption of the Constitution, *To the Democratic Voters of the State of New York*, Committee Publication no. 14 (Albany, 1915). This publication listed nineteen prominent Democrats who supported the constitution. In addition, another Committee publication (*Reasons for Democratic Support*, Committee publication no. 7 [Albany, 1915]) reprinted the speeches delivered in the Convention by Delancey Nicoll and Morgan J. O'Brien explaining their affirmative votes on the constitution.

[28]Gustavus Myers, *The History of Tammany Hall*, with an Introduction by Alexander B. Callow (N.Y.: Boni and Liveright, Inc., 1917; reprint ed., N.Y.: Dover Publications, Inc., 1971), p. 2.

[29]See, as an example, Frederick C. Tanner to the chairmen of all county committees, October 20, 1915, Frederick C. Tanner Papers.

[30]Walter T. Arndt, "The Defeated New York Constitution," *National Municipal Review* 5 (January 1916):97.

[31]Tanner, 2:161.

[32]Henry L. Stimson to Israel T. Deyo, October 28, 1915, Henry L. Stimson Papers.

[33]Frederick C. Tanner to Robert S. Binkerd, October 29, 1915, Frederick C. Tanner Papers.

[34]Henry L. Stimson to Israel T. Deyo, November 3, 1915, Henry L. Stimson Papers.

[35]One exception, by his own account, was Tanner, who wrote after the convention that he had privately urged submission in separate groups of amendments rather than submission as a whole (Tanner, 2:152-153). But even he did not argue for separate submission in the debate on the subject on the convention floor.

[36]New York State, Constitutional Convention, 1915, *Revised Record of the Constitutional Convention of the State of New York, 1915*, 4 vols. (Albany: J. B. Lyon Co., Printers, 1915), 4:4344.

[37]Ibid., p. 4336.

[38]Ibid., p. 4349.

[39]One reorganization advocate did attempt to explain this position. This was Root, who, in an address before the Republican Club of New York in the closing days of the campaign, said:

"[The constitution] is all one comprehensive scheme. You cannot submit it section by section; it is a complete interrelated, thought-out whole, for the redemption of the government of our state from the ill-repute into which it has fallen, for doing away with the selfish playing of politics in the place of government; for the reduction of the extravagance and lavishness and lack of responsibility that has brought our expenditures up from twelve millions at the time of the last convention, to forty-two millions a year at the time of this convention; that has brought our debt up from seven millions to one hundred and eighty six millions; that has made our highways and our canals and public works generally the vehicles for graft and robbery of the public" (Elihu Root, "A Study of the Proposed Constitution," address delivered to the Republican Club of New York, October 18, 1915, in *Addresses on Government and Citizenship* [Cambridge: Harvard University Press, 1916], pp. 221-222).

But this was hardly an adequate explanation. The only item in the constitution which represented a "comprehensive scheme" and "inter-related thought-out whole" aimed at the "redemption of government" from the ills Root cited was reorganization. At most, Root was making a good case for the joint submission of the two reorganization amendments, not the submission of the entire constitution as a whole!

[40]John Lord O'Brian, *The Reminiscences of John Lord O'Brian* (New York: Columbia University Oral History Research Office, 1952), p. 160.

[41]Ibid., p. 158.

[42]Henry L. Stimson to Charles F. Taylor, November 9, 1915, and to Frank B. Kellog, November 10, 1915, Henry L. Stimson Papers.

[43]Jacob Gould Schurman to C. F. Taylor, November 16, 1915, Jacob Gould Schurman Papers.

[44]Several scholars have written that it was this experience with submission by the 1915 Constitutional Convention which led to the decision of the next convention, held in 1938—the 1916 proposal to hold a constitutional convention was voted down—to submit its constitution in nine separate sections rather than as a whole (see W. Brooke Graves, *American State Government*, 3rd ed. [New York: D. C. Heath and Co., 1946], p. 102, and Ruth R. Kessler, "An Analysis of Constitutional Change in New York State," *New York University Quarterly Review* 16 [November 1938]:105).

[45]McGeorge Bundy and Henry L. Stimson, p. 76.

[46]Elihu Root to Fred W. Hammond, December 3, 1915, Elihu Root Papers, U.S. Library of Congress, Washington, D.C.

[47]See Jane S. Dahlberg, *The New York Bureau of Municipal Research, Pioneer in Government Administration* (New York: New York University Press, 1966), p. 111, n. 17.

[48]New York Bureau of Muncipal Research, "Responsible Government," *Municipal Research*, no. 69 (January 1916), p. 19.

[49]Margaret C. Alexander, *The Development of the Power of the State Executive With Special Reference to the State of New York*, Smith College Studies in History, no. 3 (Northampton, Ma.: Smith College, 1917), p. 223.

[50]Robert S. Binkerd, *The Reminiscences of Robert S. Binkerd* (New York: Columbia University Oral History Research Office, 1949), p. 75.

[51]McGeorge Bundy and Henry L. Stimson, pp. 77-78.

[52]Committee for the Adoption of the Constitution, *Why the Constitution Should be Adopted*, Committee Publication no. 3 (Albany, 1915).

[53]Walter T. Arndt, p. 97.

[54]Charles H. Crennan, *A Survey of State Executive Organization and A Plan of Reorganization* (Menasha, Wisconsin: George Banta Publishing Co., 1916), pp. 74-75.

In closing this section on the reasons behind the defeat of the constitution, mention should be made of one imponderable factor. The vote on the constitution was an expression of the way the adult male population of New York State felt about the document; women did not get the vote in New York until 1917. While there is no evidence which suggests that the distribution of their vote, had they voted, would have been appreciably different from that of the male vote, the possibility is worthy of mention in any complete review of the reasons behind the defeat of the constitution.

[55]Henry L. Stimson to Paul Shipman, November 9, 1915, Henry L. Stimson Papers. See, also, Henry L. Stimson to Edward M. Angell, William A. Breed, Robert W. deForest, Israel T. Deyo, and James Inglis, November 9, 1915, Henry L. Stimson Papers, and Elihu Root to Fred W. Hammond, December 3, 1915, Elihu Root Papers.

Chapter 5

Afterword

The debate and discussion in the convention and in the campaign for ratification created a new popular awareness of the issue of reorganization. No longer was attention to the problems and possibilities of reorganization limited to a small circle of reformers; these problems and possibilities now became the subject of discussion among large numbers of ordinary citizens throughout the state. More than just creating a popular awareness, though, the debate and discussion began a process of public education on the necessity of reorganization. This process continued for the next decade and culminated in the passage by the voters of each of the three original reorganization measures. The following is a summary description of the manner in which the short ballot, consolidation of administrative agencies, and executive budget ultimately became law.

REORGANIZATION REALIZED

One person who had become impressed with the need for reorganization through his exposure to the debates in the convention was that rising star in the Democratic party, Al Smith.[1] Upon his election to the governorship in 1918, Smith undertook to do all he could to have reorganization amendments passed. His first step was the appointment of a prestigious 35-member Commission for Reconstruction, Retrenchment and Reorganization,[2] which he

charged with studying the question of reorganization and producing specific recommendations. The commission completed its work
in October of 1919 and presented Smith with its findings and
recommendations in a lengthy, 419-page report. Among its principal recommendations were: consolidation of the state's 187[3] departments, offices, boards, and commissions into 16 central departments; reduction of the number of officials elected statewide to
include only the governor, lieutenant governor, comptroller, and
attorney general; and institution of an executive budget. Smith
accepted and endorsed these recommendations and proceeded to
urge the 1920 legislative session to approve them. The legislature's
response was to approve one amendment incorporating the first two
recommendations and to vote down another which would have
provided for an executive budget. By provision of the constitution,[4]
proposed amendments had to be approved by two separate sessions
of the legislature not having the same Senate before they could be
put to the voters for their final approval or rejection. Thus, even the
amendment passed by the legislature had before it a long and
difficult route.

As it happened,the route was to be even longer and more difficult
than expected, as Smith lost his 1920 bid for reelection to Republican Nathan Miller in that year's national Republican landslide.
Miller was no friend of reorganization and he opposed both first
passage of the executive budget amendment and second passage of
the short ballot and consolidation of agencies amendment. Neither
of the amendments was passed during Miller's two-year tenure as
governor.

In 1923, Smith was returned to the governor's office and he
wasted no time in regenerating the fight for reorganization. In a
special message to the legislature, he exhorted the legislators to
approve reorganization amendments. Once again the legislature
responded positively to a short ballot-consolidation amendment but
failed to pass an executive budget amendment. The following year,
in the legislative session of 1924, repassage of the short ballot-
consolidation amendment was finally attained, and in 1925 the
amendment was put before the electorate and gained popular
approval. Approval of the amendment set off a series of bitter
partisan political battles over the manner in which the consolidation should take place, that is, which departments, offices, boards,
and commissions should be subsumed under which central departments. To settle the bickering, Smith, in conjunction with the
legislature, appointed a State Reorganization Commission consisting of some 60 members and headed by the universally respected

Republican, Charles Evans Hughes, and asked it to produce a comprehensive scheme of consolidation. The commission completed its work in 1926 and the new system went into effect in January 1927.[5] Meanwhile, the executive budget amendment was defeated in successive legislative sessions from 1923 through 1925. Finally, in 1926, it was passed, and in 1927 it passed a second time. In the fall of 1927, the voters approved the executive budget amendment, and it went into effect in 1929.

On December 17, 1926, many of the delegates to the 1915 convention gathered at a reunion dinner in New York City. Referring to the realization of the short ballot and the consolidation of administrative agencies, and the progress made by the executive budget, Root spoke to the delegates with obvious, and well earned, satisfaction of the role played by the convention in these accomplishments:

> There are no worse enemies of all attempts at improving the machinery of government, in any field, state, municipal, national, international, than the people who are always in a hurry, who are dissatisfied if results are not reached today or tomorrow, who think that if they cannot on the instant see a result accomplished, nothing has been done. The process of civilization is always a process of building up brick by brick, stone by stone, a structure which is unnoted for years but finally, in the fruition of time, is the basis for greater progress. I think it makes but little difference what part of that process a man contributes his life to. I think it makes but little difference whether a man gives his life and his service to laying the foundation and building up the structure, or whether he is the man that floats a flag on the battlements and cries, "Victory!"[6]

REORGANIZATION IN OTHER STATES

Root's speech referred to the New York experience, but he could have made much the same point with reference to other states. The debate on and discussion of reorganization which was sparked by the convention was not limited to New York State. The revolutionary nature of the reorganization provided by the proposed constitution prompted debate and discussion in many other states as well. As was the case in New York, this debate and discussion helped create a new popular awareness of the issue of reorganization and began a process of public education on the necessity of reorganization in the country generally. And, as was the case in New York, this process of education culminated in a relatively short period of time in the adoption of reorganization measures by many states.

That their work had an impact on other states came as no surprise to the reorganization advocates in New York. They were aware all along that their work held implications for state government reorganization in the rest of the country. In the convention debate on the executive budget, Stimson said, in words which he would surely have applied equally to the other two reorganization measures, that:

> It must be evident to every member of this Convention that the question far transcends in importance the mere question of extravagance or economy in this particular State. The evil is one from which practically every State of the Union has been suffering. . . . This Convention meets at a time when what it does in the solution of this or any other similarly important problem cannot fail to have a most important effect upon the fiscal policy and the welfare of . . . every other State in the Union. . . .[7]

And during the campaign for ratification, the Committee for the Adoption of the Constitution claimed quite simply that, "Its [the constitution's] adoption will set a new standard of responsible State government. Its effect is national in importance."[8] This belief that what they were doing held implications for the rest of the country was based, in large part, on the substantial number of requests received by the reorganization advocates during the convention from various parts of the country for information on different aspects of reorganization, and on how the fight for reorganization was going in New York.[9] Many of these requests came to Stimson and one letter in particular, written to him after the convention, is noteworthy in that it referred to the impact of the work of the reorganization advocates in New York on the rest of the country. Writing of the defeat of the constitution, James Inglis of Detroit, Michigan, consoled Stimson in the following manner:

> I hope there may be some consolation to you in the fact that you have earned the gratitude not only of the people of your own state, but of the nation. It has seemed to me surprising what attention the work has received throughout the country, far more than any state measure which I have known of before. I have felt that you and your associates were blazing the way for the rest of the states.[10]

Inglis was right, of course. The reorganization advocates in New York were blazing the way for the rest of the country. Beginning with the consolidation of administrative agencies in Illinois in 1917,[11] state after state adopted some form of consolidation, short ballot, and executive budget. By 1929, every state but Arkansas had a budget system in which "the influence of the governor was always considerable and usually controlling."[12] By 1938, 26 states had reorganized their administrative systems along the lines of a consolidation of agencies and, in numbers of cases, a short ballot.[13] In Root's words, the convention had been laying a foundation and building up a structure which was a basis for further progress not only in New York, but also in the rest of the country.

NOTES

[1]This is not to suggest that Smith was unaware, prior to the convention, of the duplication, waste and irresponsibility in the state government. Having been an assemblyman since 1903, Smith had had many opportunities to note these features. But there is no question that Smith learned a great deal more about these ills, and more importantly, about specific possible cures, in the convention. Writing of Smith's participation in the convention, and taking off on what has often been said about Smith's substitution of an education in the Assembly for a formal college education, the authors of *A History of New York State* wrote: "If Smith went to College in the Assembly, he did his postgraduate work at the Constitutional Convention of 1915" (Harry F. Carman, et al., *A History of New York State*, rev. ed. [Ithaca: Cornell University Press, 1967], p. 395).

For a particularly good discussion of Smith's role in the convention, see Norman Hapgood and Henry Moskowitz, *Up From the City Streets: Alfred E. Smith* (New York: Harcourt, Brace and Co., 1927), pp. 100-130.

[2]Robert Caro writes that the word "retrenchment" was inserted into the commission's title at the suggestion of Belle Moskowitz, who recognized that the term would provide a clever public relations device, "connoting as it did economy and prudence" (Robert A. Caro, *The Power Broker: Robert Moses and the Fall of New York* [New York, Alfred A. Knopf, Inc., 1974], p. 95).

[3]New York Reconstruction Commission, *Report of the Reconstruction Commission of the State of New York, 1919* (Albany: J. B. Lyon Co., Printers, 1919), p. 6. Apparently 18 new agencies had been added since 1915 when, according to the joint count of the Department of Efficiency and Economy and the New York Bureau of Municipal Research, 169 had existed (see p. 10).

[4]New York, *Constitution* (1894), art. 14, sec. 1, ed. Francis N. Thorpe, *The Federal and State Constitution*, 7 vols. (Washington: Government Printing Office, 1909) 5:2735.

[5]In its final form, the number and breakdown of the central departments were not much different from the plan of the defeated 1915 constitution. Eighteen departments were provided for. They were: Executive, Audit and Control, Taxation and Finance, Law, State, Public Works, Conservation, Agriculture and Markets, Labor, Education, Health, Mental Hygiene, Charities, Correction, Public Service, Banking, Insurance, and Civil Service.

[6]Elihu Root, in an address to the reunion dinner of the delegates to the New York State Constitutional Convention of 1915, held on December 17, 1926, in New York City. Copy of address in the Henry L. Stimson Papers, Yale University, New Haven, CT.

[7]New York State, Constitutional Convention, 1915, *Revised Record of the Constitutional Convention of the State of New York, 1915*, 4 vols. (Albany: J. B. Lyon Co., Printers, 1915) 2:1633.

[8]Committee for the Adoption of the Constitution, *Why the Constitution Should be Adopted*, Committee Publication no. 3 (Albany, 1915), p. 14.

[9]Shortly after the convention, Root wrote that he had received more requests for the *Record of the Convention* from people in other states than from New Yorkers! (Elihu Root to Fred W. Hammond, December 3, 1915, Elihu Root Papers, U.S. Library of Congress, Washington, D.C.)

An interesting point about the interest generated in other states by the convention, is the observation made by both Root and Stimson that serious interest about the proposed reorganization in New York was apparently actually greater in the Western states than in New York itself! (See Elihu Root, "The New York Constitution and Representative Government," address delivered before the Economic Club of New York, October 25, 1915 in *Addresses on Government and Citizenship* [Cambridge: Harvard University Press, 1916], p. 238 and Henry L. Stimson to Colonel William Lassiter, November 13, 1915, Henry L. Stimson Papers.) Stimson offered an explanation for this curious state of affairs, writing that: "our work in the Convention was given more thoughtful attention out West, where they are not thinking so much about the war, than it was in our own state." (Ibid.)

¹⁰James Inglis to Henry L. Stimson, November 4, 1915, Henry L. Stimson Papers.

¹¹Illinois' was a statutory reorganization, not one accomplished by constitutional amendment. In large part, the reason a constitutional route was not sought was because of New York's experience with such an attempt. Pro-reorganization legislators in Illinois feared that some of the same reasons that caused New York voters to vote down the 1915 constitution, could be present in Illinois in 1917. (See E. O. Phillips of the Chicago Tribune to Frederick C. Tanner, February 1, 1917, Frederick C. Tanner Papers, Columbia University, New York, N.Y.) The first constitutional reorganization was accomplished in Massachusetts, in 1918.

¹²Leonard D. White, *Trends in Public Administration* (New York: McGraw-Hill Book Co., Inc., 1933), p. 334.

¹³Arthur E. Buck, *The Reorganization of State Governments in the United States* (New York: Columbia University Press, 1938), pp. 7-8.

Selected Bibliography

ARTICLES

Ager, George W. "Executive Aggression." *Atlantic Monthly*, November 1908, pp. 577-584.

Arndt, Walter T. "The Defeated New York Constitution." *National Municipal Review* 5 (January 1916):92-101.

Bates, Frank G. "Reorganization of State Administration." *American Political Science Review* 9 (May 1915):317-322.

Beard, Charles A. "Reconstructing State Government." *New Republic* 4 (August 21, 1915):1-16.

_____. "The Ballot's Burden." *Political Science Quarterly* 24 (December 1909):589-614.

_____. "The Budgetary Provisions of the New York Constitution." *The Annals of the American Academy of Political and Social Science* 62 (November 1915):64-68.

_____. "The New York Constitutional Convention." *National Municipal Review* 4 (October 1915):637-645.

Benjamin, G. G. "The Attempted Revision of the State Constitution of New York." *American Political Science Review* 1 (February 1916):20-43.

Blauvelt, George A. "The Work of the Constitutional Convention." *The Cornell Law Quarterly* 1 (November 1915):19-26.

Blue, Leonard A. "Recent Tendencies in State Administration." *The Annals of the American Academy of Political and Social Science* 18 (November 1901):434-445.

Bradford, Gamaliel. "Reform of Our State Governments." *The Annals of the American Academy of Political and Social Science* 4 (June 1893):883-903.

Bromage, Arthur W. "State Reorganization." *National Municipal Review* 24 (December 1935):665-714.

137

Buck, A. E. "Budget Progress in New York, New Jersey, and Massachusetts." *American Political Science Review* 12 (August 1918):521-530.

Burton, John. "Budget Administration in New York State." *State Government* 16 (October 1943):205-207.

Carlisle, John N. "The Proposed New Constitution." *Motordom,* October 1915, pp. 2-3.

Childs, Richard S. "New York State Reorganizes." *National Municipal Review* 15 (May 1926):265-269.

――――――. "The Short Ballot." *The Outlook* 92 (July 17, 1909):635-639.

――――――. "The Short Ballot Movement and Simplified Politics." *The Annals of the American Academy of Political and Social Science* 64 (March 1916):168-171.

Coker, F. W. "Dogmas of Administrative Reform." *American Political Science Review* 16 (August 1922):399-411.

Crawford, Finla G. "Administrative Reorganization in New York State." *American Political Science Review* 21 (May 1927):349-359.

――――――. "New York State Reorganization." *American Political Science Review* 20 (February 1926):76-79.

――――――. "The Executive Budget Decision in New York." *American Political Science Review* 24 (May 1930):403-408.

Dawson, Edgar. "The Invisible Governor and Administrative Efficiency." *The Annals of the American Academy of Political and Social Science* 64 (March 1916):11-30.

Dodd, Walter F. "Proposed Reforms in State Government Organization." *American Political Science Review* 4 (May 1910):243-251.

――――――. "Reorganizing State Government." *The Annals of the American Academy of Political and Social Science* 113 (May 1924):161-172.

――――――. "State Administrative Reorganization in New York." *American Bar Association Journal* 12 (July 1926):455-457.

Edwards, William H. "A Factual Summary of State Administrative Reorganization." *The Southwestern Political and Social Science Quarterly* 19 (June 1938):53-67.

――――――. "Has State Reorganization Succeeded." *State Government* 2 (October 1938):183-184, 192-193.

――――――. "The Public Efficiency Experts." *The Southwestern Political and Social Science Quarterly* 10 (December 1929):301-312.

Fairlie, John A. "State Administration in New York." *Political Science Quarterly* 15 (March 1900):50-74.

――――――. "The Executive Power in the State Constitution." *The Annals of the American Academy of Political and Social Science* 181 (September 1935):59-73.

――――――. "The State Governor." *Michigan Law Review* 10 (March 1912):370-383; (April 1912):458-475.

Ford, Henry J. "The Cause of Political Corruption." *Scribner's Magazine* 490 (January 1911):54-61.

Gitterman, J. M. "The Council of Appointment in New York." *Political Science Quarterly* 7 (March 1892):80-115.

Gruenberg, Frederick P. "The Executive vs. the Legislative Budget." *National Municipal Review* 7 (March 1918):167-173.

Gulick, Luther. "Effective State Government: A Problem of Organization." *State Government* 12 (June 1939):99-100, 109-110, 113.

Hamlin, Frank. "New York Constitutional Convention." *Yale Law Journal* 4 (June 1895):213-222.
Hines, Walker D. "Our Irresponsible State Governments." *Atlantic Monthly*, May 1915, pp. 637-647.
Hyneman, Charles S. "Administrative Reorganization: An Adventure into Science and Theology." *Journal of Politics* 1 (February 1939):62-75.
Jacobson, J. M. "Evaluating State Administrative Structure—the Fallacy of the Statistical Approach." *American Political Science Review* 22 (November 1928):928-935.
James, Herman G. "Reorganization of State Government." *American Political Science Review* 9 (May 1915):294-303.
Kessler, Ruth R. "An Analysis of Constitutional Change in New York State." *New York University Law Quarterly Review* 16 (November 1938):101-113.
Lapp, John A. "State Administration and Budget: Governor's Messages." *American Political Science Review* 9 (November 1916):727-732.
Ludington, Arthur. "Progress of Short Ballot Movement." *American Political Science Review* 5 (February 1911):79-83.
Lyon, Frances D. "New York State Constitutional Conventions." *New York History* 20 (January 1939):51-59.
McGoldrick, Joseph D. "Governor Smith Introduces the Cabinet in New York State." *National Municipal Review* 16 (April 1927):226-229.
Mathews, John M. "State Administrative Reorganization." *American Political Science Review* 16 (August 1922):387-398.
————. "The New Role of the Governor." *American Political Science Review* 6 (May 1912):216-228.
————. "The New Stateism." *North American Review* 193 (June 1911):808-815.
Moore, Frank C. "Constitutional Conventions in New York State." *New York History* 38 (January 1957):3-17.
Mosher, Frederick C. "The Executive Budget Empire State Style." *Public Administration Review* 12 (Spring 1952):73-84.
New York Bureau of Municipal Research. *Municipal Research* nos. 61-64, 69-70, 90-91.
Pardee, John S. "Government Running Wild." *The Outlook* 3 (November 10, 1915):618-622.
Putney, Bryant. "Reorganization of State Governments." *Editorial Research Reports* 1 (May 23, 1938):295-310.
Roosevelt, Franklin D. "Results in New York State Vindicate Administrative Reorganization." *National Municipal Review* 19 (April 1930):223-225.
Schurman, Jacob Gould. "The New Constitution for the State of New York." *The Cornell Law Quarterly* 1 (November 1915):1-18.
Sherman, Harvey M., and White, Leonard D. "The Governors March On." *State Government* 13 (October 1940):195-197, 206.
Smith, Alfred E. "How We Ruin Our Governors." *National Municipal Review* 10 (May 1921):277-280.
Spicer, George W. "Relation of the Short Ballot to Efficient Government and Popular Control." *The Southwestern Political and Social Science Quarterly* 11 (September 1930):182-192.
Stimson, Henry L. "The Essence of the Revised Constitution of New York State." *The Economic World* 10 (October 16, 1915):495-497.

Tying, Theodosius S. "A Draft of a Frame of Government." *Political Science Quarterly* 27 (June 1912):193-214.

Updyke, Frank A. "State Budgets." *American Political Science Review* 8 (February 1914):57-63.

Young, William H. "The Development of the Governorship." *State Government* 31 (Summer 1958):178-183.

Walker, Harvey. "Theory and Practice in State Organization." *National Municipal Review* 19 (April 1930):249-254.

White, Francis H. "The Growth and Future of State Boards and Commissions." *Political Science Quarterly* 18 (December 1903):631-656.

Wickersham, George W. "The New Constitution and the Work of the Bureau of Municipal Research." *The Real Estate Magazine* 6 (October 1915):15-20.

Wilson, Woodrow. "Hide-and-Seek Politics." *North American Review* 191 (May 1910):585-601.

Woodruff, Clinton R. "The Complexity of American Governmental Functions." *Political Science Quarterly* 15 (June 1900):260-272.

BOOKS

Abernathy, Bryon R. *Some Persisting Questions Concerning the Constitutional State Executive.* Lawrence, Kansas: The University of Kansas Publications Governmental Research Series no. 23, 1960.

Alexander, De Alva S. *A Political History of the State of New York.* vol. 4. New York: H. Holt and Company, 1906.

Alexander, Margaret C. *The Development of the Power of the State Executive, With Special References to the State of New York.* Smith College Studies in History, no. 3. Northampton, MA: Smith College, 1917.

Allen, William H. *Al Smith's Tammany Hall.* New York: Institute for Public Service, 1928.

Bates, Frank G., and Field, Oliver P. *State Government.* New York: Harper and Bros., 1928.

Beard, Charles A. *American Government and Politics.* 8th ed. New York: The MacMillan Co., 1939.

Bradford, Gamaliel. *The Lesson of Popular Government.* 2 vols. New York: The MacMillan Co., 1899.

Bromage, Arthur W. *State Government and Administration in the United States.* New York: Harper and Bros., 1936.

Bryce, James. *The American Commonwealth.* 2 vols. New York: The MacMillan Co., 1893; reprint ed., 1912.

Buck, Arthur E. *Budget Making.* New York: D. Appleton and Co., 1921.

————. *The Reorganization of State Governments in the United States.* New York: Columbia University Press, 1938.

Buck, Arthur E., and Cleveland, F. A. *The Budget and Responsible Government.* Introduction by William Howard Taft. New York: The MacMillan Co., 1920.

Bundy, McGeorge and Stimson, Henry L. *On Active Service in Peace and War.* New York: Harper, 1948.

Caldwell, Lynton K. *The Government and Administration of New York.* New York: Thomas Y. Crowell, 1954.

Carman, Harry F.; Ellis, D. M.; Frost, J. A.; and Syrett, H. C. *A History of New York State.* revised ed. Ithaca: Cornell University Press, 1967.

Chester, Alden. *Legal and Judicial History of New York.* vol. 2. New York: National Americana Society, 1911.

Childs, Richard S. *Civic Victories.* New York: Harper and Bros., 1952.

————. *Short Ballot Principles.* Cambridge, MA: Houghton Mifflin Co., 1911.

Cleveland, Frederick A. *Organized Democracy.* New York: Longman, Green, and Co., 1913.

Committee for the Adoption of the Constitution. *Publication.* nos. 1-17. Albany, 1915.

Crawford, Finla G. *Administrative Reorganization in New York State.* Syracuse: Syracuse University Press, 1925.

————. *State Government.* New York: Henry Holt and Co., 1931.

Crennan, Charles H. *A Survey of State Executive Organization and A Plan of Reorganization.* Menasha, Wisconsin: George Banta Publishing Co., 1916.

Croly, Herbert. *The Promise of American Life.* New York: The MacMillan Co., 1909; reprint ed., Cambridge, MA: Harvard University Press, 1965.

Dahlberg, Jane S. *The New York Bureau of Municipal Research.* New York: New York University Press, 1966.

Dodd, Walter F. *State Government.* New York: The Century Co., 1922.

Dougherty, J. Hampden. *Constitutional History of the State of New York.* 2nd ed. New York: Neale Publishing Co., 1915.

Fairlie, John A. *The Centralization of Administration in New York State.* vol. 9. Columbia University Studies in History, Economics and Public Law. New York: Columbia University, 1897.

Finley, John H., and Sanderson, John F. *The American Executive and Executive Methods.* New York: The Century Co., 1908.

Flick, Alexander C., ed. *History of the State of New York.* 10 vols. New York: Columbia University Press, 1935. vol. 7: *Constitutional Developments 1867-1915,* by Finla G. Crawford.

Ford, Henry J. *The Cost of Our National Government.* New York: The Columbia University Press, 1910.

————. *The Rise and Growth of American Politics: A Sketch of Constitutional Development.* New York: The MacMillan Co., 1898; reprint ed., 1914.

Friedman, Jacob A. *The Impeachment of Governor William Sulzer.* New York: Columbia University Press, 1939.

Gosnell, Harold F. *Boss Platt and His New York Machine.* Chicago: University of Chicago Press, 1924.

Graves, W. Brooke. *American State Government.* 3rd ed. New York: D. C. Heath & Co., 1946.

Greene, Evarts B. *The Provincial Governor in the English Colonies of North America.* vol. 7. Cambridge: Harvard Historical Studies, 1898; reprint ed., New York: Russell & Russell, 1966.

Haines, Charles G. *The Movement for the Reorganization of State Administration.* Texas: University of Texas Bulletin no. 1848 dated August 25, 1918, actually published April, 1920.

Hapgood, Norman, and Moskowitz, Henry. *Up From the City Streets: Alfred E. Smith.* New York: Harcourt, Brace and Co., 1927.

Heady, Ferrel. *State Constitutions: The Structure of Administration.* New York: National Municipal League, 1961.

Hennessy, John A. *What's the Matter With New York?* New York: The O'Connell Press, 1916.

Hill, Henry W. *Development of Constitutional Law in New York State.* Buffalo: The Peter Paul Book Co., 1896.

Hoar, Roger S. *Constitutional Conventions, Their Nature, Powers and Limitations.* Boston: Little, Brown, and Co., 1917.

Holcombe, Arthur N. *State Government in the United States.* New York: The MacMillan Co., 1916.

Hughes, Charles Evans. *Addresses and Papers of Charles Evans Hughes.* New York: G. P. Putnam's Sons, 1908.

Jameson, J. Franklin. *An Introduction to the Study of the Constitutional and Political History of the States.* Johns Hopkins University Studies in Historical and Political Science, 4th series, no. 5. Baltimore: John Murphy and Co., Printers, 1886.

Jessup, Philip C. *Elihu Root.* 2 vols. New York: Dodd Mead & Co., 1938.

Kales, Albert M. *Unpopular Government in the United States.* Chicago: The University of Chicago Press, 1914.

Kallenbach, Joseph E. *The American Chief Executive: The Presidency and the Governorship.* New York: Harper and Row, 1966.

Leopold, Richard W. *Elihu Root and the Conservative Tradition.* Boston: Little, Brown & Co., 1954.

Lincoln, Charles Z. *The Constitutional History of New York.* 5 vols. Rochester: The Lawyers Co-operative Publishing Co., 1906.

Lipson, Leslie. *The American Governor from Figurehead to Leader.* Chicago: The University of Chicago Press, 1939.

Macdonald, Austin F. *American State Government and Administration.* New York: Thomas Y. Crowell Co., 1934.

Mathews, John M. *American State Government.* New York: D. Appleton and Co., 1924.

————. *Principles of American State Administration.* New York: D. Appleton & Co., 1917.

Morison, Elting E. *Turmoil and Tradition: A Study of the Life and Times of Henry L. Stimson.* Boston: Houghton Mifflin Co., 1960.

Myers, Gustavus. *The History of Tammany Hall.* Introduction by Alexander B. Callow. New York: Boni and Liveright, Inc., 1917; reprint ed., New York: Dover Publications, Inc., 1971.

Nevins, Allan. *The American States During and After the Revolution 1775-1789.* New York: The MacMillan Co., 1924.

Poore, Benjamin, ed. *The Federal and State Constitutions.* 2 vols. Washington: Government Printing Office, 1878.

Porter, Kirk H. *State Administration.* New York: Crofts, 1938.

Ransone, Coleman B. *The Office of Governor in the United States,* Alabama: University of Alabama Press, 1956.

Reed, Thomas H. *Government for the People.* New York: B. W. Huebsch, 1915.

Riensch, P. S. *Readings on American State Government.* Boston: Ginn & Co., 1911.

Rich, Bennett. *State Constitutions: The Governor.* New York: National
Municipal League, 1960.
Root, Elihu. *Addresses on Government and Citizenship.* Cambridge:
Harvard University Press, 1916.
Skinner, Charles R. *Governors of New York From 1777-1920.* Albany: J. B.
Lyon Company, Printers, 1919.
Smith, Alfred E. *The Reorganized State Government.* Albany: J. B. Lyon
Company, Printers, 1926.
Smith, Ray B., ed. *History of the State of New York, Political and
Governmental.* 6 vols. Syracuse, The Syracuse Press Inc., 1922. vol. 4:
*History of the State of New York, Political and Governmental,
1896-1920,* by Roscoe C. E. Brown.
Stebbins, Homer A. *A Political History of the State of New York 1865-
1869.* vol. 55. Columbia University Studies in History, Economics and
Public Law. New York: Columbia University, 1913.
Stickney, Albert. *Organized Democracy.* Boston: Houghton Mifflin and
Co.; Cambridge: The Riverside Press, 1906.
Stimson, Frederic J. *Federal and State Constitutions of the United States.*
Boston: The Boston Book Co., 1908.
Sturm, Albert L. *Methods of State Constitutional Reform.* Ann Arbor:
University of Michigan Press, 1954.
Sullivan, James. *History of New York State, 1523-1927.* vol. 5. New York:
Lewis Historical Publishing Co., Inc., 1927.
Thatch, Charles C. *The Creation of the Presidency 1775-1789.* Baltimore:
The Johns Hopkins University Press, 1923; 2nd printing, 1969.
Thorpe, Francis N., ed. *The Federal and State Constitutions.* 7 vols.
Washington: Government Printing Office, 1909.
Yellowitz, Irwin. *Labor and the Progressive Movement in New York State,
1897-1916.* Ithaca: Cornell University Press, 1965.
Weber, Gustavus A. *Organized Efforts for the Improvement of Methods of
Administration in the United States.* New York: D. Appleton and Co.,
1919.
Wesser, Robert F. *Charles Evans Hughes; Politics and Reform in New
York, 1905-1910.* Ithaca: Cornell University Press, 1967.
White, Leonard D. *Introduction to the Study of Public Administration.*
New York: The MacMillan Co., 1926.
————. *Trends In Public Administration.* New York: McGraw-Hill Book
Co., 1933.
Willoughby, William F. *Movement for Budgetary Reform in the States.*
New York: D. Appleton and Co., 1918.
————. *The Problem of a National Budget.* New York: D. Appleton and
Co., 1918.

DISSERTATIONS

Crown, James. "The Development of Democratic Government in the State
of New York Through the Growth of the Power of the Executive Since
1920." Ph.D. dissertation, New York University, 1956.

INTERVIEWS

Childs, Richard S. Brooklyn, N.Y. Interview, August, 21, 1974.
Gulick, Luther. New York, N.Y. Interview, November 13, 1974.
Marshall, James. New York, N.Y. Interview, November 22, 1974.
Spero, Sterling. New York, N.Y. Interview, July 24, 1974.

ORAL HISTORY RESEARCH OFFICE

New York, N.Y. Columbia University Oral History Research Office. William H. Allen, 1950.
————. Robert S. Binkerd, 1949.
————. Richard S. Childs, 1950.
————. John Lord O'Brian, 1952.
————. William A. Prendergast, 1951.
————. Martin Saxe, 1949.
————. Francis R. Stoddard, 1949.
————. Frederick C. Tanner, 1949-1950.
————. James W. Wadsworth, 1951.

PAPERS

Ithaca, N.Y. Cornell University, Department of Manuscripts and University Archives. Jacob Gould Schurman Papers.
New Haven, CT. Yale University Library. Henry L. Stimson Papers.
New York, N.Y. Columbia University Libraries. Seth Low Papers.
New York, N.Y. Columbia University Libraries. Herbert Parsons Papers.
New York, N.Y. Columbia University Libraries. Frederick C. Tanner Papers.
Washington, D.C. U.S. Library of Congress. Elihu Root Papers.
Washington, D.C. U.S. Library of Congress. James W. Wadsworth Papers.

PROCEEDINGS

Beard, Charles. "Tendencies Affecting the Size of the Ballot." *Proceedings of the American Political Science Association* 6. New York, N.Y.: December 27, 1909-December 31, 1909.
Childs, Richard S. "Ballot Reform: Need of Simplification." *Proceedings of the American Political Science Association* 6. New York, N.Y.: December 27, 1909-December 31, 1909.
Cleveland, Frederick A. "Constitutional Provisions For A Budget." *Proceedings of the Academy of Political Science* 5. New York, N.Y.: October 1914.
Croly, Herbert. "State Political Reorganization." *Proceedings of the American Political Science Association* 8. Buffalo, N.Y. and Toronto, Ontario: December 27, 1911-December 30, 1911.
Dodd, Walter F. "State Reorganizations and the Federal Problem." *Proceedings of the Academy of Political Science* 9. New York, N.Y. : July 1921.

_____. "The Constitutional Convention: Preliminary Work, Procedure and Submission of Conclusions." *Proceedings of the Academy of Political Science* 5. New York, N.Y.: October 1914.

Ford, Henry J. "The Reorganization of State Government." *Proceedings of the Academy of Political Science* 3. New York, N.Y.: January 1913.

Howe, Frederic C. "The Constitution and Public Opinion." *Proceedings of the Academy of Political Science* 5. New York, N.Y.: October 1914.

Lowrie, S. Gale. "Suggestions for a State Budget." *Proceedings of the American Political Science Association* 9. Boston, MA: December 28, 1912-December 31, 1912.

Ludington, Arthur. "Proposed Methods of Ballot Simplification." *Proceedings of the American Political Science Association* 6. New York, N.Y.: December 27, 1909-December 31, 1909.

McBain, Howard L. "The Problem of Governmental Reorganization." *Proceedings of the Academy of Political Science* 9. New York, N.Y.: July 1921.

Root, Elihu. "The Principles and Practice of Constitutional Revision." *Proceedings of the Academy of Political Science* 5. New York, N.Y.: October 1914.

Shaw, Albert. "The Problems of the Constitutional Convention." *Proceedings of the Academy of Political Science* 5. New York, N.Y.: October 1914.

Stimson, Henry L. "The Principle of Responsiblity in Government." *Proceedings of the Academy of Political Science* 5. New York, N.Y.: October 1914.

Young, James T. "The Relation of the Executive to the Legislative Power." *Proceedings of the American Political Science Association* 1. Chicago, IL: December 28, 1904-December 30, 1904.

PUBLIC DOCUMENTS

Illinois Efficiency and Economy Committee. *Report of the Efficiency and Economy Committee, 1915.* Chicago: Windermere Press, 1915.

New York Constitutional Convention, 1915. *Documents of the Constitutional Convention of the State of New York, 1915.* Albany: J. B. Lyon Co., Printers, 1915.

_____. *Journal of the Constitutional Convention, 1915.* Albany: J. B. Lyon Co., Printers, 1915.

_____. *Proposed Amendments of the Constitutional Convention of the State of New York, 1915.* Albany: J. B. Lyon Co., Printers, 1915.

_____. *Revised Record of the Constitutional Convention of the State of New York, 1915.* 4 vols. Albany: J. B. Lyon Co., Printers, 1915.

New York Department of Efficiency and Economy. *Government of the State of New York: A Survey of its Organization and Functions, 1915.* Albany: J. B. Lyon Co., Printers, 1915.

New York Reconstruction Commission. *Report of the Reconstruction Commission of the State of New York, 1919.* Albany: J. B. Lyon Co., Printers, 1919.

Index of Participants

147